A WALK TO THE CROSS

A 30-Day Journey to Rediscover the Awe of Jesus' Death and Resurrection

A WALK TO THE CROSS

TIM DILENA

Carpenter's Son Publishing

A Walk to the Cross: 30 Days to Rediscover the Awe of Jesus' Death and Resurrection

Published by Carpenter's Son Publishing

Carpentersonpublishing.com

Cover and Interior Design by Hybrid Studios, Inc. (hybridstudios.com)

ISBN: 978-1-956370-88-1

Printed in the United States of America

For all those who struggle with the question,
"Does God really love me?"

May *A Walk to the Cross* silence all doubt
and disbelief by clearly and undeniably showing you
that the cross is God's declaration of love
for all humanity, you included.

Romans 5:8

CONTENTS

PART THREE

THE TRIAL

PART FOUR

THE GARDEN

PART FIVE

THE CROSS

PART SIX

THE GRAVE

FINAL WORDS

INTRODUCTION

Walk with Me to These Six Places

A Walk to the Cross is a special devotional. It is not meant to be a book to give us more information on the most sacred season of the year. Instead, it is meant to prepare our souls to see afresh and anew what has been made common through redundancy.

The Paschal season has been hijacked by church-growth people who have focused more on it being the biggest draw in numbers to churches instead of being the greatest victory day for the planet. We have prepared productions instead of preparing our hearts for all that God wants to do and say to us. *A Walk to the Cross* is meant to shake us free from commercialized Christianity and awaken us invariably to the reason why Jesus came from heaven to earth.

The next thirty days can change your life. *A Walk to the Cross* is meant to be read and meditated on every day, a month before Good Friday. In this devotional journey, you will encounter six places that lead us to the greatest moment in human history: the cross and the resurrection. Walk with me to six places and your life will be changed.

My prayer is that as you walk from the Last Supper into the Garden of Gethsemane, into the Jerusalem courtroom, the journey to Golgotha, and the cross and the empty grave, you will sense something happening to you. You will feel your world, your dreams, your visions, and your ambitions all becoming smaller and smaller as you see the greatest global mission come to fruition: the redemption of humankind. I say smaller because the modern church has found a way to make us larger and larger when a true vision of God does the opposite. A better word is humility. *A Walk to the Cross* is meant to bring us to our knees before God's love and sacrifice.

For the next thirty days, you will encounter empty promises, betrayal, grievous injustices, unmitigated pain, and deathbed last words and last breaths, all leading to the most shocking plot twist, a glorious resurrection. May *A Walk to the Cross* truly revive and renew your heart for this Easter season.

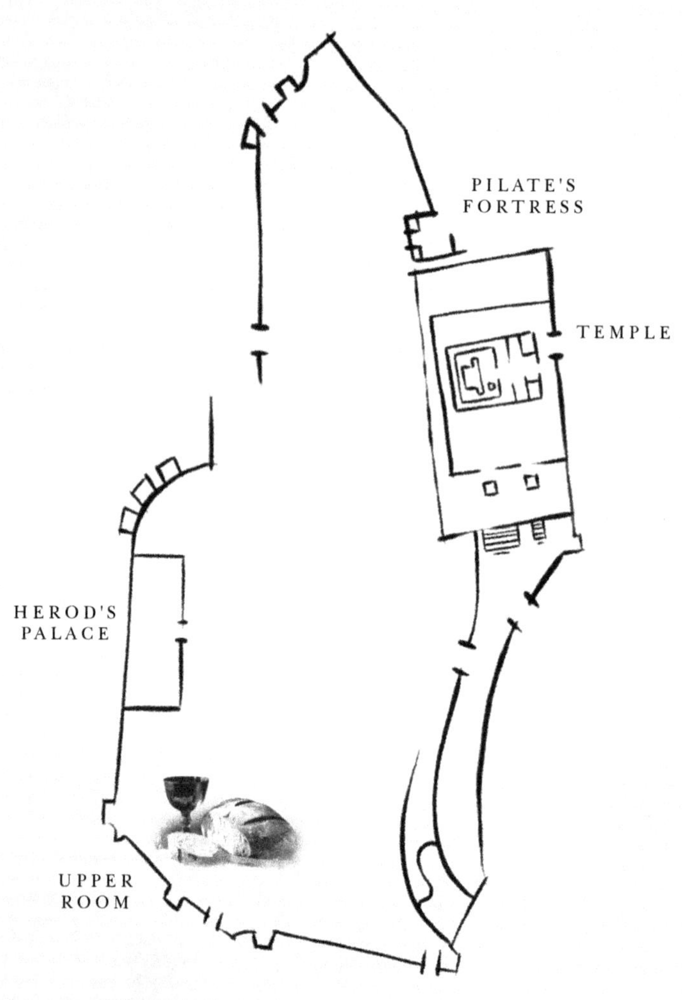
PILATE'S
FORTRESS
TEMPLE
HEROD'S
PALACE
UPPER
ROOM

PART ONE

THE SUPPER

DAY ONE

Darkness and Light

For this first communion called the Last Supper, there are two things in preparation: really, they are two forces in conflict. There are two sets of instructions being given for this meal. One is coming from Jesus, and the other is coming from Satan. One is commissioning the two disciples who saw the empty tomb first to be the first to see the upper room where this meal will take place. The other is being ordered to launch the greatest betrayal in human history. Peter and John shall get everything prepared for the upper room, and Judas will get everything prepared for a kiss in a garden. That final meal will be filled with darkness and light.

Luke shows us two simultaneous events in progress on that day in Luke 22:3–8 (NASB):

> **3** And Satan entered into Judas who was called
> Iscariot, belonging to the number of the twelve. **4**
> And he went away and discussed with the chief
> priests and officers how he might betray Him to
> them. **5** And they were glad, and agreed to give
> him money. **6** And he consented, and began seeking
> a good opportunity to betray Him to them apart
> from the multitude. **7** Then came the first day of
> Unleavened Bread on which the Passover lamb
> had to be sacrificed. **8** And He sent Peter and John,

saying, "Go and prepare the Passover for us, that we may eat it."

The words are chilling as Luke describes Judas' journey to being thirty pieces of silver richer. It was a journey toward betrayal of the most loving Being in the universe. Judas would betray Jesus.

In Luke 22:3, we read, "And Satan entered into Judas who was called Iscariot, belonging to the number of the twelve." Satan entering Judas should be enough, but it's the last phrase that disturbs the soul: "belonging to the number of the twelve." There is so much packed in those seven words.

This man heard Jesus with his own ears. Judas ate with Him and ministered with Him and saw the miracles firsthand, yet despite all of this, his soul could be entered by hell. These twelve were rounding the final lap of Jesus' mission being completed, and somehow Judas would not cross the finish line. His life would end with him hanging himself from guilt. It's always the cost of sin. The silver shines and twinkles at the beginning and then loses its luster as you take account of your decision and realize that "This is what I sold my soul for."

When Leonardo da Vinci was painting his masterpiece, the Last Supper, he searched long and hard for a model for his Christ. Legend has it that at last he located a chorister in one of the churches of Rome who was lovely in life and features, a young man named Pietro Bandinelli.

Years passed, and the painting was still unfinished. All the disciples had been portrayed save one—Judas Iscariot. Now, he began the quest to find a man whose face was hardened and distorted by sin—and at last he found a beggar on the streets of Rome with a face so villainous, he shuddered when he looked at him.

He hired the man to sit for him as he painted the face of Judas on his canvas. When he was about to dismiss the man, he said, "I have not yet found out your name."

"I am Pietro Bandinelli," he replied, "I also sat for you as your model of Christ."

The bigger question is, can this happen to me? Can I be in church, sing songs, and be labeled with a denomination only to find myself taking a turn at the end? Can I look like Christ and Judas in my lifetime?

Every day, we face the battle to listen to Christ's instructions or Satan's lies. There is a betrayer and a disciple in all of us. I can only be a disciple with the help of The Helper, the Holy Spirit. Each day we have to commit ourselves to the assignment of Christ. Thirty pieces of silver and religious agendas are always calling me away from the great work, the work for Christ.

MY PRAYER FOR TODAY

Father, today I choose You. With Your help, I willingly say yes to Your instructions and no to man's fraudulent appeals. I know my eyes can see the silver coins, but let me always remember the end of sin. I want a life that looks like Christ. I want a life that will always look like Christ. At the end of my life, may no one mistake me for the betrayer at the Last Supper.

DAY 2

God's Strange Google Map Route

A man carrying a pot of water will kickstart the greatest event in human history. Nothing could be stranger to the Jerusalem eye than this sight. Men never did that kind of work: it was always reserved for the women. Why was a man carrying a water pot in the first place? Was his wife sick? Was he one of those men who wanted to help his family any way he could even if it meant being a public spectacle? No one knows.

But what we do know is that God would make this oddity Google Maps for Peter and John. That curious sight would get them heading in the right direction where the Last Supper would take place.

When Peter and John asked Jesus where they were supposed to prepare the Passover meal, never did they expect Jesus' GPS to give these directions. Luke 22:10–13 (NASB) says,

> **10** And He said to them, "Behold, when you have entered the city, a man will meet you carrying a pitcher of water; follow him into the house that he enters. **11** And you shall say to the owner of the house, 'The Teacher says to you, "Where is the guest room in which I may eat the Passover with My disciples?"'

12 And he will show you a large, furnished, upper
room; prepare it there." 13 And they departed and
found everything just as He had told them; and they
prepared the Passover.

Sometimes, God will use the strange to get our attention. Sometimes, God will use the strange to get us walking in the right direction. Peter and John would see a man with a water pot, and then somehow a homeowner would prepare a large upper room without knowing what he was preparing it for and for Whom he was preparing it for. A man with a water pot and a man with a furnished room would be Google Maps.

Augustine is considered to be one of the greatest conversions and theological minds in Christendom. He was knee-deep into sin but had a praying mother. Who would've thought that a little child on the other side of a wall saying, "Take it and read it; take it and read it," would be the start of his conversion and impact in the church.

Upon hearing the child, Augustine picked up what was nearby, Paul's Letter to the Romans, and began reading Romans 13:13–14. This started the journey of one of the greatest Christians. His man with a water pot was a singing child.[1]

For John Wesley, his man with a water pot and man with a furnished room was a group of singing Christians on a boat in a storm. They were called the Moravians. While Wesley was coming to America to convert the Indians, he realized he had no peace if he was to die on this ship in the storm, but these Moravians did. Their joy and peace in the middle of the storm is what captured Wesley's heart and started his journey. He realized at the moment he was not a believer, though he was in ministry. He wrote in his journal, “I went to America to convert the Indians; but oh, who shall convert me?”[2]

God will use the strange to catch our attention. Look for men with water pots, singing children in Milan, and people singing on a boat in a storm. What may seem odd to the natural eye may actually be God getting our attention to put us on the path toward redemption.

The apostle Paul prayed a prayer that “the eyes of our hearts” (see Ephesians 1:18) would be enlightened to see differently. Before you snicker, label, or shake your head at the peculiar or unfamiliar, readjust the eyes of your heart, and you just may have directions to a place you have never been before. Nothing stranger would be seen and misdefined than a man on the cross dying for the whole world. And that dying man would be God’s Google Map to heaven.

MY PRAYER FOR TODAY

Lord, give me new eyes to see more clearly. Help me to see with the eyes of my heart before I define events and people with the eyes of my head. If You are trying to get my attention today to bring me to a new place, help me to follow the directions, even if the path looks unusual and out of my comfort zone. Maybe the very person You are wanting me to follow is looked upon as strange to others.

Let me not miss the man with a water pot.

1. Augustine, of Hippo, Saint, 354-430, *The Confessions of Saint Augustine,* trans. Edward B. Pusey, "The Eighth Book" (New York: P F Collier & Son, [c1909]), 141. See also https://www.ccel.org/ccel/augustine/confessions.xi.html.

2. John Wesley, *John Wesley's Journal (As Abridged by Nehemiah Curnock),* "The Voyage to England" (Werrington, Peterborough, Cambridgeshire, England: Epworth Press, 1949), n.p. *See also Journal of John Wesley,* "The Voyage to England," https://www.ccel.org/ccel/wesley/journal.vi.ii.vii.html#:~:text=%22I%20went%20to%20America%2C%20to,To%20die%20is%20gain!'.

DAY 3

Transparency vs Honesty Determines Betrayal

You must be honest with everyone and transparent with those you trust. Honesty is nonnegotiable. You must be honest with a coworker, a spouse, and even the government. Anything less is lying.

Transparency is something different. That is where you share your "beyond the truth." You share your soul. People get to look into your heart. The people I am honest with can hurt me, but the people I am transparent with can betray me.

Hurt turns into betrayal when transparency is not guarded and protected. Jesus was honest with everyone, and Jesus was transparent with twelve disciples. He shared His heart and soul and mission with them behind closed doors. There was no place more sacred than this meal in an upper room. It is at this table that Jesus reveals that there will be a betrayal.

Mark 14:18–21 (NLT) tells the story like this:

> **18** As they were at the table eating, Jesus said, "I
> tell you the truth, one of you eating with me here will
> betray me." **19** Greatly distressed, each one asked in
> turn, "Am I the one?" **20** He replied, "It is one of
> you twelve who is eating from this bowl with me.
> **21** For the Son of Man must die, as the Scriptures
> declared long ago."

But how terrible it will be for the one who betrays Him.

Some years ago, it happened to me. I don't know what I was thinking except that I was young in the ministry and naive. There was a leader in the church who sat with me and confessed some sins in his life. After he did that, he said, "You know my struggles, and in order for us to be friends, you have to tell me some struggle you are having."

There is train wreck written all over that request. While you are shaking your head no, I said yes for whatever reason. With no exaggeration to the rest of the story, soon after, I had people coming to me saying, "We heard about your struggle, and we are praying for you."

If I could be honest, it wasn't an issue of "what was said" but "who said it." That's where betrayal becomes real.

David bares his soul on his betrayal story. Read how he describes the "who" in Psalm 55:12–14 (NASB):

> **12** For it is not an enemy who reproaches me,
> Then I could bear it;
> Nor is it one who hates me who has exalted himself against me,
> Then I could hide myself from him.
> **13** But it is you, a man my equal,
> My companion and my familiar friend;
> **14** We who had sweet fellowship together,
> Walked in the house of God in the throng.

The name Judas will forever be associated with his betrayal of the Son of God. David had a Judas. I have to believe that many of you reading this have gone through your betrayal moment with someone not stewarding your transparency.

We don't know the name of David's betrayer, but what we do know is his proximity. The Message paraphrase gives some teeth to verses 13–14:

> **13** It's you! We grew up together!
> You! My best friend!
> **14** Those long hours of leisure as we walked
> arm in arm, God a third party to our conversation.

Judas did not have horns and a pitchfork. Judas didn't look like a betrayer because none of the others said, "Is it Judas?" For three years he walked with Jesus and heard Jesus share His heart and soul. Judas didn't let Jesus' transparency change him; instead, he used Jesus' transparency as a bargaining tool to make thirty pieces of silver.

People don't make money on betrayal today, but they do gain some short-term currency. By betraying confidence, you want people to admire you because you have inside information. You want people to like you because you gave them information that they never had. That's currency.

Before Jesus would go through the agonizing night of prayer in the Garden of Gethsemane, and before He would suffer the mocking and crucifixion, Jesus would suffer a deeper pain that would go underneath His skin. Jesus would experience betrayal from a man He personally called disciple and called friend (see Matthew 26:50).

Betrayal carries soul pain. It carries with it thoughts of revenge and retaliation. It's been said that intimacy is proportional to hurt. I have to believe that Judas' betrayal was more deeply felt than the mocking of strangers at the bottom of the cross, because Judas was close.

Betrayal is God's curriculum to bring massive growth to

our lives. It carries with it a soul wound that can only be healed by forgiving the betrayer and blessing the betrayer—two things that seem impossible in the middle of the offense but are necessary to scour the soul from darkness. Anyone who takes up their cross daily will be in harm's way of betrayal because it's part of the cross walk.

MY PRAYER FOR TODAY

Father, I choose forgiveness instead of revenge. I choose blessing over retaliation. Each time the betrayer's face comes to mind, I will forgive and bless them. When my mind starts running my Last Supper betrayal over and over again, please give me the strength to think higher thoughts. Help me to think Christlike thoughts all the time knowing that all of us have that capacity to betray inside of us.

DAY 4

What I Learned About Preaching from the Last Supper

The two worst days of my life in the beginning of ministry and preaching had always been Saturday and Monday. It was on Saturday that I was struggling all day to find a verse, an illustration, or a thought to share with the people that would show up at church to see and feel all my hard work. And these were pre-internet days, so I would have twenty-five books spread out all over my floor just to find one nugget of truth.

The second worst day was Monday. After I had the time to let the damage I caused on Sunday sink in, it then became a depressing day of "no one was changed, saved, or transformed and even cared." And then, the icing on the cake was "I got to do this again for the midweek service?" Then it became full-fledged depression. "There has to be a better way," is what I thought. And over the years, I found one.

It all depended upon what my "h" looked like.

Let me explain . . .

There is a familiar story in the Gospel of John that has so changed my life on preparing for the sermon on

Sunday. It's the story of the Last Supper. But it's more than sermon prep.

Jesus and the disciples are together when Peter wonders what Jesus meant when He said, "One of you will betray me." What I love about Peter is that he is always asking the question that everyone is thinking but is afraid to ask. But "who" he asks is what set me on my journey. Let John 13:23–26 (NASB) speak for itself:

> **23** There was reclining on Jesus' bosom one of His disciples, whom Jesus loved. **24** So Simon Peter gestured to him, and said to him, "Tell us who it is of whom He is speaking." **25** He, leaning back thus on Jesus' bosom, said to Him, "Lord, who is it?" **26** Jesus then answered, "That is the one for whom I shall dip the morsel and give it to him."

Follow the process here in the passage. The one "reclining on Jesus' bosom" is John, the writer of this Gospel. Then Peter signals to "him" (small h) and said to "him" (small h) to ask Jesus who He is talking about. Next, notice verse 25. Here is where "it" happens. The one leaning on the bosom of Jesus said to "Him" (the big "H"), "Lord who is it?" And then it says in verse 26, "Jesus then answered. . . ."

This exchange is amazing. Peter hears something from the Second member of the Godhead. He doesn't understand it. So who does he ask?

Therein, to me, lies the secret. It's the secret of sermon preparation, preaching with authority, and freedom from sermon depression. It's the "h" issue: Peter spent his time asking John to ask Jesus, instead of asking Jesus himself.

Think of where John is. He is leaning on the breast or

the bosom of Jesus. His head is resting on His chest. That means John is hearing the heartbeat of God.

Just the surface thought of that is staggering. To lean on the breast of Jesus is to get the heartbeat of Jesus. John hears what makes His heart beat faster and gets Him excited, per se. But Peter, like most of us, has learned to ask "the leaners on the breast of Jesus" what the answers are instead of trying to find a spot on His chest himself.

There are sermons and then there is God's heart. For the precious people I preach to every Sunday at Times Square Church in New York City, I want to deliver God's heart to them.

Over my four decades in the ministry, I have spent most of my life asking the little "h" what God meant, and now I am finally learning to ask the big "H."

I think Luther's axiom carries more weight with me than ever: "He who has prayed well has studied well."[1]

I am not pleading with preachers not to be well studied. I am pleading with them to get back to a vacant spot that some have abdicated for something lesser. I am pleading with pastors to come back to the breast of Jesus and hear Him, the big "H."

I know the difference when I have listened to a well-studied man and a well-prayed man. The man who first starts with the little "h" can craft a masterpiece of a sermon. Every point can start with "P," and it can be an alliteration that should be viral. But there is something about the man who hears Jesus' heartbeat first. That pastor speaks with authority.

My plea is to hear His heart first before anything else.

Always remember that there is a vacant spot on the bosom of Jesus waiting for you. He wants you to place your ear there to hear what saddens His heart and what makes it glad. The heartbeat of God is heard in prayer.

This is not a lesson for preachers only; this is a lesson for all of us. In this age of technology, the little "h" has multiplied exponentially. Everyone wants your attention, your "like," and your view: they want you friending them or following them so they can be that little "h" voice in your life. This is a time for Christians to get back to the heart of Jesus. It's time for us to hear what Christ is saying.

Every time you see Leonard da Vinci's painting of the Last Supper, I want you to see it differently. I want you to be focused on the two people to Jesus' left: it's John and Peter. John is next to Jesus and Peter is next to John. Peter is speaking to John, it seems, just before John is about to speak to Jesus. When I see the painting, I don't want to interact with John; I want to switch places with John.

And here is the good news: you can.

MY PRAYER FOR TODAY

Father, it seems every day I have to fight to be in John's place because it is so easy to be in Peter's position. It's a fight to hear Your heart but a worthy one. Voices are crying out for my attention constantly, but help me to hear Your heart above the noise. Hearing Your heartbeat will make all the difference. It's not to preach better sermons, it's to be a better son and daughter.

1. E. M. Bounds, *The Complete Works of E.M. Bounds on Prayer Quotes, 7th ed.* (New Kensington, PA: Whitaker House, 1997), Kindle.

DAY 5

A Fight Broke Out at the Last Supper

I can't believe the disciples were arguing about this at the Last Supper. A fight broke out at the Last Supper. Not with fists but with words.

The disciples had just had communion. The disciples had just heard about a betrayer in their midst. And right after these two giant topics, an argument happens at the table where they just took the bread and wine, and its topic was, "Who's the greatest?" This is how it went in Luke 22:24–26 (NLT):

> **24** Then they began to argue among themselves
> about who would be the greatest among them. **25**
> Jesus told them, "In this world the kings and great
> men lord it over their people, yet they are called
> 'friends of the people.' **26** But among you it will be
> different. Those who are the greatest among you
> should take the lowest rank, and the leader should
> be like a servant."

Jesus had to redefine greatness to these men who had no sense of the solemnity of the moment and the ridiculousness of the moment all happening together.

Jesus told the disciples that there is a competing set of

definitions for greatness. Jesus continued to give them clarity on greatness being connected with serving.

He says in Luke 22:27, "Who is more important, the one who sits at the table or the one who serves? The one who sits at the table, of course. But not here! For I am among you as one who serves."

The challenge is that men are fighting to get a seat instead of serving the seated.

Jesus essentially says that we want to be serving those seated at the table. In serving is greatness. I don't think it's an accident that "leader" is mentioned only six times in the Bible and "servant" is mentioned over nine hundred times.[1]

We hear about a lot of "leader conferences," but I think we need to get more "servant conferences." Greatness is wrapped up in that word "servant." Look for the men who serve, and you will find the most important person in the room per Jesus' definition.

Gary Inrig tells us why D.L. Moody was great in his book, *A Call to Excellence*:

"A large group of European pastors came to one of D.L. Moody's Northfield Bible Conferences in Massachusetts in the late 1800s. Following the European custom of the time, each guest put his shoes outside his room to be cleaned by the hall servants overnight. But, of course, this was America and there were no hall servants.

"Walking the dormitory halls that night, Moody saw the shoes and determined not to embarrass his brothers. He mentioned the need to some ministerial students who were there but was met with only silence or pious excuses. Moody returned to the dorm, gathered up the shoes, and, alone in his room, the world's only famous evangelist began to clean and polish the shoes. Only the unexpected arrival of a friend in the midst of the work revealed the secret.

"When the foreign visitors opened their doors the next morning, their shoes were shined. They never know by whom. Moody told no one, but his friend told a few people, and during the rest of the conference, different men volunteered to shine the shoes in secret.

"Perhaps the episode is a vital insight into why God used D.L. Moody as He did. He was a man with a servant's heart and that was the basis of his true greatness."[2]

Moody later said, "There are many of us that are willing to do great things for the Lord, but few of us are willing to do little things."[3]

MY PRAYER FOR TODAY

Father, please forgive me for believing other men's definitions. Forgive me for believing that greatness is found in the man that is sitting at the table instead of the man who shines shoes. You were clear that our greatest pursuit is to serve. Teach me to be a servant even if I don't like shining shoes.

1. Tony Cooke, "Is Leadership Teaching Scriptural?" Tony Cooke Ministries, accessed February 17, 2025, https://tonycooke.org/articles-by-tony-cooke/leadership-teaching-scriptural/.

2. Gary Inrig, *A Call to Excellence* (Wheaton, IL: Victor Books, 1985), 98.

3. D.L. Moody Center, "The Quotable Moody," MoodyCenter.org, accessed February 10, 2025 https://moodycenter.org/the-quotable-moody-d-l-moody-quotes/.

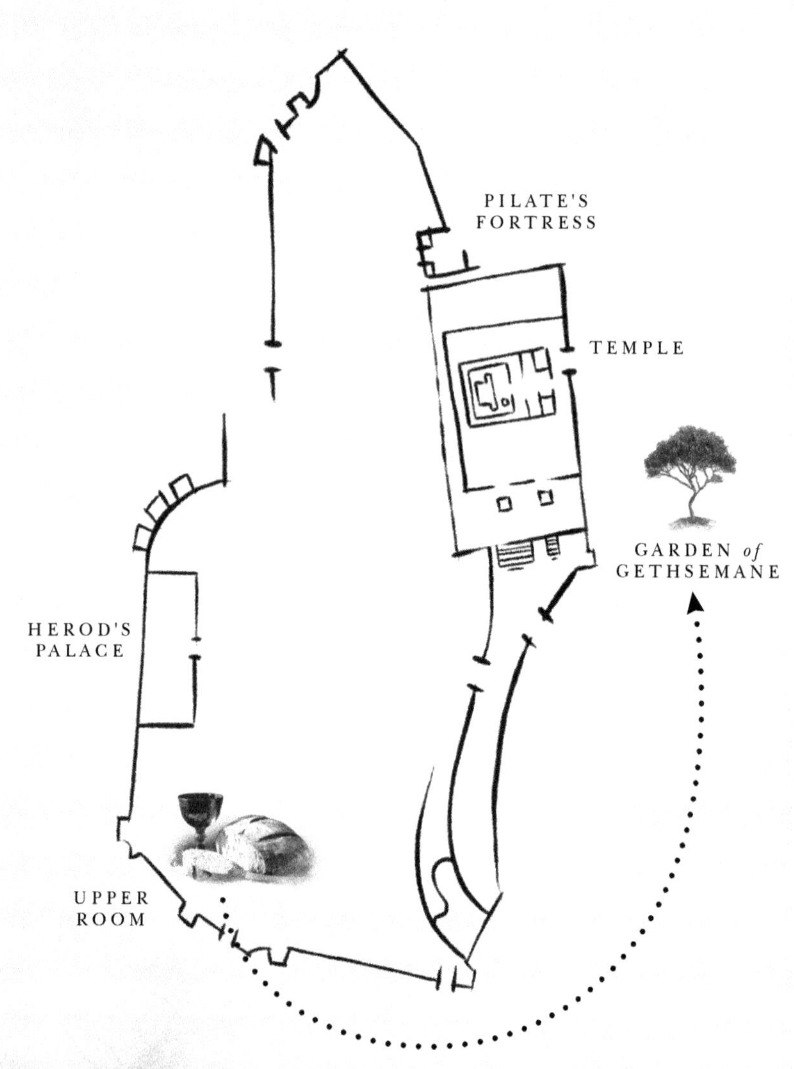
PILATE'S
FORTRESS
TEMPLE
GARDEN *of*
GETHSEMANE
HEROD'S
PALACE
UPPER
ROOM

PART TWO

THE GARDEN

DAY 6

Cup Decisions Are Made Beyond

Of all the places that make up the walk to the cross, it's the garden that gets overlooked and minimized. This is where the fight was. This is the place that helped Jesus deal with the past betrayal and the future brutal beatings and suffering because it's the place where Jesus says yes to God's will. It's also a sacred place because you see the battle with "the cup."

The cup represents the will of God. The contents of the cup represent the suffering and the pain to do His Father's will. We get to see the humanity of Jesus when He, in anguish, asks that if possible, may the cup be forgone in this mission. The garden showed us the spiritual fight to do the will of God.

There are three "thems" in the garden. Look for it in Matthew 26:36–39 (NASB):

> **36** Then Jesus *came with them to a place called
> Gethsemane, and *told His disciples, "Sit here while
> I go over there and pray." **37** And He took Peter and
> the two sons of Zebedee with Him, and began to be
> grieved and distressed. **38** Then He *said to them,
> "My soul is deeply grieved, to the point of death;
> remain here and keep watch with Me." **39** And He

> went a little beyond them, and fell on His face and prayed, saying, "My Father, if it is possible, let this cup pass from Me; yet not as I will, but as You will."

The first "them" is the twelve disciples in verse 36. They all went to Gethsemane together. The second "them" is in verse 38: it's Peter, James, and John. It would be those three who would hear and see the battle of the soul of Jesus to do the will of God.

Jesus left the twelve and then He left the three; the only "them" that is left is Jesus and His Father. Though the word is not used, we see clearly the two of them speaking.

Don't miss the words "a little beyond them." Those are the words that bring separation from voices of friends and influencers, and now it's you and God. He is the Influencer.

The three disciples that Jesus loved and Jesus would pick to come into the most memorable places like the transfiguration, the raising of the little girl behind closed doors, and now, in the Garden of Gethsemane, those three are forbidden to cross this threshold. It was holy ground. It was to be one on one between The Son and The Father. That's a journey we all must make.

To go "a little beyond" is the place of private prayer. It's the place where private prayer becomes a struggle to do the will of God. It's where the soul becomes honest and becomes real. It happened to Jacob at Jabot where he wrestled with the angel of the Lord.

This may offend you, but let these words sink into your soul: if you don't have a time "a little beyond" between you and Jesus, it's hard to believe that you are doing the will of God. It is in those "beyond" times where we are presented with "the cup" and asked to do the hard things. The contents of that cup may be a humbling apology to a spouse, a generosity sacrifice, or it just may be the leaving of a career for a calling.

Our churches need more prayer meetings. Our families need more prayer around the table. But this is a call to "beyond." This is where the struggle and the victory come from. It's when you go beyond "them"—beyond the family and the Church family to decide regardless of what you're being asked, the answer is, "Yes, Father."

Before there were *Star Wars* sagas and host of other space movies, there was the original *Star Trek*. And every Friday night, your TV would have a dark screen, and you would see outer space and hear this monologue from William Shatner: "Space: the final frontier. These are the voyages of the starship Enterprise. Its five-year mission: to explore strange new worlds, to seek out new life and new civilizations, to boldly go where no man has gone before."[1]

You could superimpose Shatner's opening word and change it from "space" to "prayer." Gethsemane prayer is going beyond "them." It's a mission to go where no one can go except you.

MY PRAYER FOR TODAY

Father, I love the noise in the company of life, and it becomes uncomfortable when it's gone and I hear nothing. I know how needful it is for me to get alone with You. It's easy to leave the twelve, a little more difficult to leave my three, but the challenge of my life is to find time for You alone. The enemy will do whatever it can to keep me from going a little bit beyond because the enemy doesn't want me to make the hard decisions about the cup.

Let me start today going beyond.

1. See "Where no man has gone before," *Wikipedia*, last modified November 24, 2024, https://en.wikipedia.org/wiki/Where_no_man_has_gone_before.

DAY 7

The Very Day I Call for Help, the Tide of the Battle Turns

Make no mistake, Jesus' prayer in the Garden of Gethsemane is what enabled Him to do the will of God, the walk to the cross. The will of God was full of suffering and pain, but it was prayer that allowed Jesus to say yes.

It was the wife of martyr Jim Elliot, Elizabeth, who said, "The will of God is not something you add to your life. It's a course you choose. You either line yourself up with the Son of God . . . or you capitulate to the principle which governs the rest of the world."[1]

Doing the will of God and daily prayer are inseparable. Without prayer, there is no resounding yes to the will of God. Without prayer, we can miss knowing the will of God.

In Acts 10, we are introduced to the will of God and a praying man. His name is Cornelius, the Italian centurion. He is known as a man of prayer.

It says Cornelius "prayed regularly to God" (see Acts 10:2 NLT). It would be during one of those times of prayer that a visitation from God would come which would lead this Italian to meet a Jew who would change all of our lives. He was to take a journey to Joppa and meet the disciple Peter and invite him to come back to Caeserea to preach salvation and pray over his household. The Holy Spirit fell on those Gentiles that day, which the church leaders said was like a Pentecost for the Gentiles. It happened because an Italian prayed and obeyed.

I have to believe there was a battle that Cornelius faced to go to Joppa and interact with a Jew. There was no love lost between these two people groups. How does this man win the fight over community racism and stereotyping? Prayer wins that fight.

This has to be one of the most powerful verses I discovered in the last year. It's Psalm 55:6 from The Living Bible. It describes what happened in the Garden of Gethsemane and in Caesarea. The Psalmist says in Psalm 56:9, "The very day I call for help, the tide of battle turns. My enemies flee! This one thing I know: God is for me!"

The tide turned on the battle. Hell gets pushed back. This is what happened to Cornelius, and this is what happened to Jesus. The prayer of the garden turned the tide of the battle.

Just as Cornelius probably did not want to take the walk from Caesarea to Joppa, Jesus had the fight with His walk from Gethsemane to Jerusalem. The flesh was put under His feet. The grieving, distressed soul of the Son of God was now filled with peace and joy for what was set before Him. Prayer turned the tide of the battle. His dialogue with God gave him the strength to drink the cup and to say yes. Prayer always turns the tide of the battle.

When you are at a crossroads of doing the will of God, don't weigh the options. Fall on your knees and cry out to God! You will know what to do next. God will give you the courage to take the walk. The tide of the battle that is raging in your soul will turn, the enemy will flee, and you will know God is for you.

But I must tell you, it's in those times that we will not have a lot of words to express ourselves. Jesus just had one sentence, but that's all that was needed. He said, "My Father, if it is not possible for this cup to be taken away unless I drink it, may your will be done" (Matt. 26:42 NIV).

When I'm on my knees at a crossroads, I remember the great words of the nineteenth-century English preacher J. C. Ryle: "Fear not because your prayer is stammering, your words feeble, and your language poor. Jesus can understand you."[2]

MY PRAYER FOR TODAY

Father, when I am at a crossroads of not knowing what to do, so many times I fail because all I do is weigh my options instead of falling on my knees. Here I am today, God, saying to You, "Not my will but Your will be done." When I am standing at the crossroads, I'm seeing what benefits me most. But when I am on my knees at a crossroads, I'm saying, "What gives You the most glory?" Help me choose glory over comfortability. Turn the tide of the battle within me.

1. See "Elizabeth Elliot > Quotes > Quotable Quote," goodreads, accessed February 22, 2025, https://www.goodreads.com/quotes/350456-the-will-of-god-is-not-something-you-add-to.

2. J. C. Ryle, *A Call to Prayer, 2nd ed.* (Ovilla, TX: Heritage Bible Fellowship, 2011), Kindle.

DAY 8

Three's a Charm

There has been this silly notion that a true prayer of faith is prayed only one time. Nothing could be further from the truth, especially from the teaching and example of the life of Jesus. His prayer in the garden proves that Jesus lived what He taught. He prayed this way in the garden because of what He believed and taught from a mountain. In the Sermon on the Mount, Jesus said, in Matthew 7:7–8 (NIV),

> **7** Ask and it will be given to you; seek and you will
> find; knock and the door will be opened to you. **8** For
> everyone who asks receives; the one who seeks finds;
> and to the one who knocks, the door will be opened.

The original language of this passage is insightful. It is a present-tense imperative. Jesus wasn't challenging us to knock, seek, or ask once. He was imploring us to make it a continuous act of keep on seeking, keep on knocking, and keep on asking. That is exactly what happened in the Garden of Gethsemane. For Jesus, three times was a charm.

The phrase "three's a charm" more than likely came from some superstitious belief. For a person who believes in luck, it was that number of times someone could find their pot of gold.

To be clear, Jesus wasn't operating on luck. He believed that whoever kept seeking would find; whoever kept knocking, it would be open to them; and whoever kept asking, there would be an answer. Jesus prayed the same prayer three times, and a breakthrough came. When Jesus broke from the disciples in Matthew 26:42–44 (NASB), this is what happened:

> **42** He went away again a second time and prayed, saying, "My Father, if this cannot pass away unless I drink it, Thy will be done." **43** And again He came and found them sleeping, for their eyes were heavy. **44** And He left them again, and went away and prayed a third time, saying the same thing once more.

It seems that this third time was a charm. Jesus gets up and seems to go from deep grief and struggle into resolve and focus. Something happened to Jesus. He heard from heaven, and He got His answer. The answer was, "God's will, will most assuredly be done and the cup of suffering would not pass from Him." That was all Jesus needed to move forward.

Notice how resolute He was in Matthew 26:45–46:

> **45** Then He came to the disciples, and *said to them, "Are you still sleeping and taking your rest? Behold, the hour is at hand and the Son of Man is being betrayed into the hands of sinners. **46** Arise, let us be going; behold, the one who betrays Me is at hand!"

Jesus knew what was ahead, He knew what He had to face, and He was now ready. He is ready for the betrayer.

He is ready to go meet the Roman soldiers and start the journey to the cross. He is ready for the scourging and the mocking. He is ready to forgive and invite a thief to heaven. He is ready to face hell and commission His disciples with a great commission. He is ready to ascend and sit at the right of the Father.

Charles Finney is considered to be the greatest American evangelist of all time. They say that 85 percent of his converts remained true to Christ . . . ten years after their conversion.[1]

I was reading about his journey to salvation. He had a hunger for God but never surrendered to God. He would regularly go to church just because of the Gladstone's law book he was reading: it had so many quotes from the Bible that he wanted to hear about it in the church.

Finney attended a prayer meeting at a church even though he wasn't a Christian. What was sobering was that Finney was going to a prayer meeting as a heathen, and we can't even get Christians to show up for a prayer meeting!

His biographer said this, "Finney was now regularly attending the weekly prayer meeting and the thing that struck him most was that the people who prayed never got their prayers answered. In fact, it seemed to him that they did not expect to get their prayers answered, yet when he searched the Bible [which he was now doing almost constantly], he found an abundance of Scriptures in which God promised to answer prayers. . . ."[2]

He added, "On one occasion when I was in one of the prayer meetings, I was asked if I did not desire that they should pray for me! I told them, no; because I did not see that God answered their prayers. I said, 'I suppose I need to be prayed for, for I am conscious that I am a sinner; but

I do not see that it will do any good for you to pray for me; for you are continually asking, but you do not receive.'"[3]

Isn't that amazing? The heathen wouldn't let the Christians pray for him because they didn't get their prayers answered. It was the most crucial moment of the Son of God's life, and He needed His prayer answered . . . and it was. What He taught three years earlier would take three times to pray and then a breakthrough occurred. I believe God answers prayer and I believe it's okay to keep knocking, God will open that door wide.

Don't give up: for Jesus, three's a charm.

MY PRAYER FOR TODAY

Father, don't let me give up believing that You answer prayer. Help me to keep seeking and keep knocking and keep asking. I know the number of times is not the secret as man would make us think. Jesus praying three times was a challenge to not give up. I am still knocking for salvation for loved ones. I will continue to ask for healing for friends. I will continue to seek for a fresh anointing from God every day.

1. J. Gilchrist Lawson, *Deeper Experiences of Deeper Christians* (CreateSpace, 2016), as excerpted in The Gospel Truth, "Charles G. Finny: A Brief Biography," GospelTruth, accessed February 14, 2025, https://www.gospeltruth.net/lawsonbio.htm.

2. Ibid.

3. Ibid.

DAY 9

Praying with Your Eyes Open

The Garden of Gethsemane became an epicenter of prayer before the most monumental moment in human history, man's redemption. The movement of the Son of God into this powerful moment would be obviously opposed by hell. There would be a fight to stop Him, but prayer would be the weapon to overcome for the Son of Man. Prayer would be His choice weapon, and we are instructed it would be the weapon for every believer.

To fight through obstacles, we must pray. To fight distractions for God's goals, we must pray. But then Jesus surprises the reader by adding a new dimension to the prayer life. Jesus speaks to His disciples about the power of temptation and tells them that in order to fight temptation, they need to pray with their eyes open.

Any praying man must be the watching man. They must watch who they keep company with, where they go, what they listen to, and where they let their minds wander. Jesus said in Matt 26:41 (NASB), "Keep watching and praying, that you may not enter into temptation; the spirit is willing, but the flesh is weak."

Prayer gives us the power to say no to temptation, but it is "watching" that is the mechanism to keep us from being irresponsible with that power. Watching helps us not to provoke the Lord. That means we ask for victory but then carelessly put our souls in a temptation place. We may say as a married man, "Lord, help me love my wife as Christ loves the church." That is a great and biblical prayer. Every husband should pray that prayer.

Let's add to that prayer some "watching."

Let's say that your team at the job has just successfully completed a deal or a project and everyone wants to celebrate. In order for the success to have happened, there was a lot your family sacrificed by not seeing you many nights. Your team is wanting to go out and party. You are now finding out that your first prayer is going to need spiritual eyes.

This is adding "watching" to your prayer. This is where you realize that this is not the best place for me, my marriage, my children, or my reputation. There could be temptation of all sorts in that venue. This is praying with your eyes open. Answering, "No thanks, I will head home to my family," is victory.

How do we watch and pray? Maybe we should ask, "How do I become a 'watcher'?" There are so many books and conferences on how to pray, but no one teaches us how to watch so we don't fall into temptation. I think the "watcher's" main response is, "No, thank you." They know when to say no. Watchers start to see possible temptation ground so that they may avoid it.

I believe that prayer keeps us very sensitive to dangerous places. Prayer helps the alarms go off in a conversation and even an invitation. Prayer flips the switch on seeing with new eyes. Prayer helps us see things for what they really are and not as they are portrayed. This is called discernment. I believe watching carries with it discernment and decisiveness.

In Luke 11:1, the disciples beseeched Jesus for profound guidance, saying, "Lord, teach us how to pray."

Luke 11 is Prayer 101. Jesus follows up with the Lord's Prayer. The words are memorized and quoted all over the world today.

But let's not forget the Prayer 201 lesson from the Gethsemane Garden. This is where the Lord teaches how to watch and pray that we may not enter into temptation. This is where Jesus instructs us to pray with our eyes open.

MY PRAYER FOR TODAY

Father, after I get off my knees from praying, I ask You to flip the switch on and help me to see with new eyes today. Help me to watch my steps, my words, my going in, and my going out. I thank You that You have given me the strength to overcome a weak flesh. I don't want to find myself in any relationship, in any conversation, or in any place that You are not pleased with. Teach me how to pray like the disciples asked, but also teach me how to pray with my eyes open.

DAY 10

Finding Myself in the Highly Emotional Will of God

I have learned over the years that being in the center of God's will can also be an emotional roller coaster. In fact, I have learned that the will of God carries many emotions with it.

I don't think there is a place in the Gospels that shows Jesus' humanity more than the Garden of Gethsemane. Jesus is right where He needs to be. He was supposed to be in the garden after the Last Supper and before His mock trial. It is in that garden that He will be readied by prayer for the next horrific twenty-four hours of His earthly life.

We see an emotional Jesus, whereas the bulk of the Gospels have Jesus moving in peace, power, and poise. There is a fight happening. There is an internal struggle that is boiling. Jesus is in the fight of His life but in the highly emotional will of God.

This insight of the emotions of Jesus is recorded in Matthew 26:36–38 (NASB):

> **36** Then Jesus *came with them to a place called Gethsemane, and said to His disciples, "Sit here while I go over there and pray." **37** And He took with

> Him Peter and the two sons of Zebedee, and began
> to be grieved and distressed. **38** Then He *said to
> them, "My soul is deeply grieved, to the point of
> death; remain here and keep watch with Me."

There is grief, distress, and even deep grief upon Jesus. Let those words sink in. He is in the right place with an internal emotional fight.

The Garden of Gethsemane is the place of prayer before the journey to the cross. But this prayer closet is emotional ground. And the lesson we see here is invaluable.

There is something in us that believes when we are doing what God wants us to do, we have nothing but joy and singing. Well, let me burst your bubble: nothing could be further from the truth. The will of God can be an emotional roller coaster. Always remember that emotions are not the indicator of being in the right place: it is having God's peace.

I must have the peace of Christ in the will of God. Peace will keep me steady. Emotions will bounce me around. I make decisions based on peace, not emotions. When I am sad, it doesn't mean I move. When I am happy, it doesn't mean it's right. When I am angry or hurt, that is not a signal to pack my bags.

Emotions are not God's providence. If it was, Jesus is leaving the Garden of Gethsemane before He even starts to pray. It would take the Son of God going back to His knees three times to get peace and resolve that He wasn't veering off but staying on course.

I am fascinated with Jonah, the prophet who took a ride in a big fish because he wouldn't go to Nineveh to preach. He went off course but eventually made it back to the place where God initially wanted him to go. Because the big fish is looming in Jonah's story, it's easy to let other things take a back seat. It's his final chapter that is revelatory.

In Jonah 4, the prophet is in Nineveh, the right place, but inundated with so many different emotions. In verse 1, Jonah is angry. In verse 3, he feels suicidal. Then Jonah is happy in verse 6. He is exhausted in verse 8. The chapter ends with Jonah angry again in verse 9. All of these emotions after a successful Nineveh revival while in the will of God.

This is a huge reminder that we can have peace and a host of emotions at the same time. And it is that heavenly peace that keeps the emotions in check, as Paul tells us in Philippians 4:7: "And the peace of God, which surpasses all comprehension, will guard your hearts and your minds in Christ Jesus."

When we walk in peace, we may be emotional, but we will walk in obedience. Elisabeth Elliot says it best in her book *Discipline: The Glad Surrender*: "It is Christ who is to be exalted, not our feelings. We will know Him by obedience, not by emotions. Our love will be shown by obedience, not by how good we feel about God at a given moment."[1]

We are people submitted to the will of God. We will not surrender and be directed and dictated by emotions.

MY PRAYER FOR TODAY

Father, today may be emotional, but let there be a peace that passes understanding to guide me and steady me (Col 3:15). There are moments I may be hurt, I may get angry, and I may even be happy, but keep me steady in Your will. I know Your will is where I want to be. There may be a lot going on internally inside, but I surrender to You despite the roller coaster.

1. Elisabeth Elliot, *Discipline: The Glad Surrender* (Ada, MI: Revell, 1982), 148.

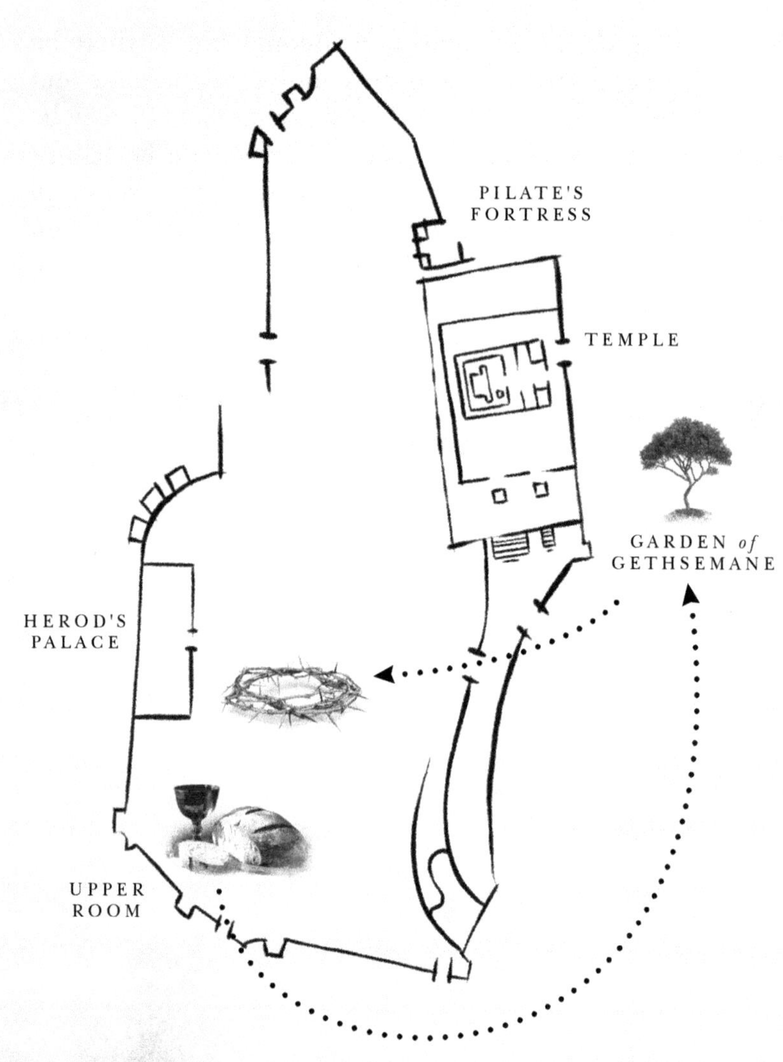
PILATE'S
FORTRESS
TEMPLE
GARDEN *of*
GETHSEMANE
HEROD'S
PALACE
UPPER
ROOM

PART THREE

THE TRIAL

DAY 11

I've Never Told This Story Before

I don't think I ever told this personal story before. The reason may be from embarrassment, or it may be that it still incites something inside me. It was small from a bystander's perspective but highly humiliating to the victim.

I was the victim. It happened at a denominational event backstage. I really don't think anyone witnessed it.

I arrived early to get ready to do my part of this citywide event. The director was a nice man but sometimes would cross boundaries in word and deed. His boundary crossing was nothing ever egregious or ever had an effect on me. People would just say when he ventured across the line, "That's just so-and-so."

But this day, his line crossing shocked me. It may not even sound like a big deal, but it did make Jesus' trial a little bit more real to me.

The gentleman came up in a playful manner and said something to the effect of, "Dilena, about time you made it!" But what came next was startling.

He took his rolled-up program for the night and hit me on my forehead. That was it. Even writing it has some emotion to it.

To the first-time reader, it may seem minuscule and playful, but there is something highly demeaning and humiliating to this act. It seemed to me it was as if he used his title and position to show me he was in a power position over me. I know that may seem a bit much. I am just telling you how it felt to have a man take a rolled-up piece of paper and tap me on the head like I was an animal that was being corrected.

I am telling you that Mark 15:19 (NASB) always evokes emotion in me when I read it. The gospel writer says, "And they kept beating His head with a reed, and spitting at Him, and kneeling and bowing before Him."

They kept beating His head with a reed. I cringe when I read it. I felt one soft tap, and I was humiliated. I am appalled at this verse and feel it. It's a verse to the natural eye that may not bring much emotion, but to me, it does.

There are certain happenings in life that bring both external pain and internal pain. The hitting of the King of kings on the head with a reed may not engender the external pain from what a crown of thorns or a scourging causes, but there is an internal pain that goes along with it.

The hitting Him on his head was going after His soul. The soldiers were essentially telling Jesus that we are in the position of power and You are not. Whether these were blows or taps on the head, it was going after the very core of Jesus. They were mocking His Person. They were ridiculing His title. They were trying to discredit Who He was.

What does reed hitting have to do with me? I believe we miss the internal pain of the cross. That internal pain is what happened at the trial of Jesus. Calvary will be horrendous and a pain beyond human comprehension. It is the trial that has the element of going beyond the ripping of the flesh to the ripping of the soul. It's us understanding that Jesus understands all of our pain. It's realizing that the cross was not just external but internal.

The bogus trial of Jesus reminds us that corrupt men in authority positions will abuse the soul. Sometimes, that pain is more devastating than an external hurt.

What is the answer to the internal assault? Peter gives us the answer in what Jesus did. It's tucked away in 1 Peter and is easy to miss.

I wonder if Peter witnessed the head tapping with the reed and somehow realized this answer. Peter said in 1 Peter 2:23 (TPT): "When he was verbally abused, he did not return with an insult; when he suffered, he would not threaten retaliation. Jesus faithfully entrusted himself into the hands of God, who judges righteously."

That's it! Jesus faithfully entrusted Himself into the hands of God, Who judges righteously. I did not do that, but I must do that. I give it to God to set things right, starting first with my soul.

MY PRAYER FOR TODAY

Father, I can't believe that I still have emotions in my soul from something that occurred decades ago. It just shows how fragile my soul is. I have faced other moments of reed tapping in my life. Maybe not with a piece of paper, but it was an assault on my soul. I have learned and will entrust myself to my Father who judges righteously.

My life is in Your hands.

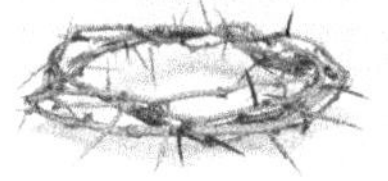

DAY 12

The Danger of Hyperbole

Never say "never," and always stay away from the word "always." Those words have made many people liars. I have told God before: "I will never worry again, God . . . I will always trust You, Lord." Well, that's just impossible!

These words have been used in marital conversations and marital fights. These are bad fighting words: "You never pick up your clothes" or "You never say I love you" and "You always leave the dishes." Those statements are just not true. Here is why: "Always" and "never" are God words. Those words describe utter consistency. We are not consistent creatures; only God is.

Hebrews 13:8 (KJV) says this about God, "He is the same yesterday, today and forever." The last book of the Old Testament reminds us of this attribute of God in Malachi 3:6, "I am the Lord, I change not."

This attribute is called the immutability of God.

Remember, we are always changing.

God never does!

Peter broke this rule. He used "never." He declared himself immutable. Peter took on God attributes when he said at the Last Supper in Matthew 26:31–33 (NASB):

> **31** Then Jesus said to them, "You will all fall away
> because of Me this night, for it is written, 'I will
> strike down the shepherd, and the sheep of the flock
> shall be scattered.' **32** But after I have been raised, I
> will go ahead of you to Galilee." **33** But Peter said to
> Him, "Even though all may fall away because of You,
> I will never fall away."

Jesus quickly warned Peter that his "never" was impossible; he would deny Him, and the signal of this would be a rooster crowing. It took less than twenty-four hours to prove Peter was not immutable.

While Jesus is being spit on and beaten and told to prophesy the person who hit Him, Peter is outside the halls just moments away from three denials, a rooster crowing, and a cry of defeat. It says this in Matthew 26:69–75:

> **69** Now Peter was sitting outside in the courtyard,
> and a servant-girl came to him and said, "You too
> were with Jesus the Galilean." **70** But he denied it
> before them all, saying, "I do not know what you
> are talking about." **71** When he had gone out to the
> gateway, another servant-girl saw him and *said to
> those who were there, "This man was with Jesus of
> Nazareth." **72** And again he denied it with an oath, "I
> do not know the man." **73** A little later the bystanders
> came up and said to Peter, "Surely you too are one
> of them; for even the way you talk gives you away."
> **74** Then he began to curse and swear, "I do not
> know the man!" And immediately a rooster crowed.
> **75** And Peter remembered the words which Jesus
> had said, "Before a rooster crows, you will deny Me
> three times." And he went out and wept bitterly.

Peter goes from "I will never fall away" to "I never knew Him" in twenty-four hours!! While Jesus is being beaten and mocked, Peter is outside the trial doors, failing miserably.

Here is what we learn about Peter's really messy twenty-four hours. When we become big, God gets small. I hate the inconsistencies in my life because I really think of myself as amazing, but it's just not true. So how do I make myself big? It's called carnival mirrors. Rather than humbly standing before the honest assessment of the mirror of the Bible to see myself as I really am, I look into carnival mirrors.

The problem with the carnival mirror is that it does show you, but your image is distorted. Carnival mirrors make you large. You don't actually have a 20-inch-high neck and a 6-inch torso. Yes, it's you in that concave mirror, but it's not showing you the way you actually look.

We are all attracted to overinflated, aggrandized views of ourselves. To use Paul's words, we think of ourselves "more highly than we ought to think" (see Romans 12:3). We all want to be seen as right and mature. We all want to be looked up to and esteemed. So we all are susceptible to having our definition of ourselves formed by the carnival mirrors. Remember, when we get big, God gets small, and He becomes something lesser than us.

The two greatest revelations you can have in life is that there is a God, and you are not Him. We put upon ourselves God terms. We say, "I've always tried to do what's right" and "I would never hurt anyone."

That's impossible because you are not God. Peter walked with the real Jesus for three years and still got it wrong. So when you make yourself big and God becomes small, it's a recipe for disaster and failure!

Christian author Tony Campolo told the story where he once was confronted by an atheist who was one of his students at the university where he was a professor. The young man told Campolo, "For me to believe in God, I have to have a God that I can understand." To which Campolo tersely replied, "God refuses to be that small!"[1]

Evelyn Underhill, a nineteenth-century English author, summed it up this way, "If God were small enough to be understood, He would not be big enough to be worshiped."[2]

MY PRAYER FOR TODAY

Father, I want to be on record today to say, "I am not You and I will never be You and I will always need You." Please forgive me for my hyperbole living. I have fallen into this Peter trap and experienced the Peter failure. I will let Your Bible be the mirror today. I will not let society and people be my mirror. You are big and I am small. I need a Big God today to face this big world.

1. Tony Campolo, *Let Me Tell You a Story: Life Lessons from Unexpected Places and Unlikely People* (Nashville: Thomas Nelson, 2000), Kindle.

2. Evelyn Underhill, as quoted in Elisabeth Elliot, *Secure in the Everlasting Arms* (Ada, MI: Revell, 2002), 91.

DAY 13

The Back and Forth of a Restless Soul

Pontius Pilate was the Roman governor of Judaea who presided over Jesus' trial in the Praetorium, but he is extremely restless. He is standing in front of the Son of God as His judge.

This thought is insane. Pilate judging Jesus. I think Pilate's soul was restless with this role. Pilate could not seem to sit still and was moving at a rapid pace in and out of the crowd. At Jesus' trial in John 18 and 19, Pilate can't seem to make a decision as to whether to defend Jesus or side with the mob. He is uneasy, and his constant movement reveals his soul.

My head is spinning when I read about Pilate. Six times, the governor is inside the Praetorium and then outside with the screaming crowd. The verse prior, a rooster has crowed, and a disciple has failed by taking the wrong side. Peter has capitulated and became part of the mob by denying Jesus.

Pilate is different. He can't seem to take any side. In John 18:28–29 (NASB), Pilate's irresolution begins:

> **28** They led Jesus therefore from Caiaphas into the Praetorium, and it was early; and they themselves did not enter into the Praetorium in order that they might not be defiled, but might eat the Passover.

29 Pilate therefore went out to them, and *said, "What accusation do you bring against this Man?"

Your head will start to spin from Pilate's wavering. Once the crowd accuses Jesus, Pilate has to talk to Jesus. In John 19:33, he is back in front of the Son of God: "Pilate therefore entered again into the Praetorium, and summoned Jesus, and said to Him, "Are You the King of the Jews?"

After hearing from Jesus, it says in verse 38, "And when he had said this, he went out again to the Jews, and *said to them, 'I find no guilt in Him.'"

Do you see his restless soul?

He is not done. In John 19, Pilate's restless soul will continue to vacillate. He leaves the crowd again and comes and sees Jesus and has Him scourged (see John 19:1). Maybe this will satisfy the crowd and give him margin to truly assess this man and why his soul is in upheaval.

Pilate comes out again to the crowd in John 19:4: "And Pilate came out again, and *said to them, 'Behold, I am bringing Him out to you, that you may know that I find no guilt in Him.'"

Pilate is thinking the whipping and my pronouncement of not guilty should be adequate. It was not to be. Pilate would not get off that easy. It got more intense because the mob started shouting, "Crucify Him, Crucify Him!" (see John 19:6). Pilate was in distress.

Look at his last movement in John 19:8–9: **8** "When Pilate therefore heard this statement, he was the more afraid;
9 and he entered into the Praetorium again, and *said to Jesus, '"Where are You from?'"

He needed answers from Jesus above the noise of the crowd. I am shocked by this high official's movement and his vacillation. He can't seem to land anywhere.

Pilate's soul is in a battle. There is something in the words of this man. And there is something about being liked by the crowd. The crowd screams and yells, but this man seems to speak with authority. Do I follow who is the loudest? Or do I follow what I think is the truth? Honestly, his eternity is in the balance. He must decide. He will decide even if he is indecisive, because his indecisiveness is still a decision.

Pilate moved back and forth six times and never could bring himself to publicly confess Christ or side with the crowd. This is the state of many people's souls. They are restless and find themselves going back and forth. They are in church one Sunday and an atheist the next. They can't let their restless heart land.

The early church writer Augustine said this, "You have made us for yourself, O Lord, and our hearts are restless until they rest in You."[1]

So stop wavering and heed the five-thousand-year-old challenge of a Jewish general when he spoke to a nation these words, "But if you refuse to serve the LORD, then choose today whom you will serve. . . . But as for me and my family, we will serve the LORD" (Joshua 24:15 NLT).

MY PRAYER FOR TODAY

Father, I choose You. When the crowds are loud, I choose You. When my flesh is screaming, I choose You. When it's easier to just do what everyone else is doing, I choose You. There is a cost to choosing You. It is worth it because You chose me two thousand years ago, and that's why Jesus came.

1. Augustine, *Confessions*, 1,1.5. See also "Lord, teach me to praise Thee," https://www.vatican.va/spirit/documents/spirit_20020821_agostino_en.html.

DAY 14

A Thousand People with the Right Words but the Wrong Heart

He was wearing a crown, holding a scepter, and was donning a robe, but it was all in fun. It was all a mockery. A whole Roman cohort gathered around Jesus, and, in their mind, gave Him "king toys to pretend." This wasn't a few bullies around the Messiah. A Roman cohort was a military unit that could have as few as 480 soldiers, but could range up to one thousand men.

The size of a Roman cohort varied over time, and it depended on the situation. The thought of a thousand soldiers gathered around a suffering Jewish rabbi and making fun of him is deplorable. It's hard to see what one bully could do to a defenseless kid, but a thousand against one is unthinkable. But what makes it more unimaginable is that this isn't a defenseless person. A thousand soldiers were saying the right thing but with the wrong heart. They have no idea Who they are saying it to and that there is coming a day that the tables will be turned. He will not be the defenseless . . . but He will be their Judge.

Matthew tells us that up to one thousand soldiers representing all different ranks, from centurions to legionaries, participated in this mock worship service. We are told in Matthew 27:27–29 (NASB):

> **27** Then the soldiers of the governor took Jesus
> into the Praetorium and gathered the whole Roman
> cohort around Him. **28** And they stripped Him, and
> put a scarlet robe on Him. **29** And after weaving
> a crown of thorns, they put it on His head, and a
> reed in His right hand; and they kneeled down
> before Him and mocked Him, saying, "Hail, King
> of the Jews!"

The Praetorium was once the palace of Herod the Great and his son, King Herod II. It was now the palace of the governor. The Praetorium also housed the Roman military governor. These grounds have seen royalty and kings. These floors have had knees touching them as soldiers greeted kings. But this middle-of-the-night parody would one day turn into a reality with the script flipped.

"Hail" was a word reserved for a king. It was never used on an ordinary person. It was a word of respect and honor. None of those things were in the Praetorium that night. There were one thousand people saying the right words with the wrong heart. They thought they were saying "hail" to an ordinary man. Make no mistake, there is coming a day that those same Roman soldiers will say the right words with the right heart. They will not just say "Hail, King of the Jews" but they will say "Hail, King of kings and Lord of lords." That day is inevitable. That day is coming. That day will happen.

I am offended and convicted by a thousand Roman soldiers. How many times have I said something about Jesus that has not been lived out in my life? What's the difference?

Whether it's a thousand voices in front of the physical body of Jesus, or whether it's me saying it in front of Jesus on heaven's throne, it's all the same . . . and it's frightening.

I don't want to be labeled with this cohort. I don't want my mouth saying things not lived out fully and passionately. When I say, "God, You have everything under control in my family," I want to mean it. When I say, "God, I trust You with this sickness," I want to mean it. When I say, "God, You tell me to forgive because I have been forgiven," I want to mean it. No longer lips and life contradicting. I don't want to be a Roman soldier; I want to be a soldier for the King of kings.

MY PRAYER FOR TODAY

Father, may my lips never speak what my heart doesn't believe. May my lips never speak things that my life never lives. That is hypocrisy, and those hypocrites were who You shared Your harshest words with. I want to be numbered with the authentic, the real, and the honest.

Start with my heart. Work deep in my soul. I want my lips to be reserved for truth. I want to say, "Hail, my King" with a servant's heart every morning.

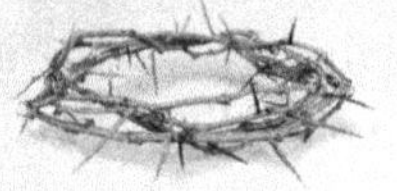

DAY 15

Now, I Understand Meekness

We are all tempted to use our power, position, and title to defend ourselves or to make ourselves seem important. Whether you are a CEO, a college professor, an airline agent, a police officer, or a retail store clerk, we all may have the upper hand many times with people. We can choose to display power, abuse power, or show meekness and power. It's those that choose meekness that inherit the earth.

The third Beatitude from the Sermon on the Mount (see Matthew 5:5 NKJV) has always puzzled me. In all honesty, it seems somewhat incongruent.

Jesus says, "Blessed are the meek for they shall inherit the earth." I would have inserted "blessed are the powerful."

This is where our understanding of meekness needs updating. I have heard it said, meekness is not weakness. The word "meekness" is best defined as "power under control." It's a person who has the title and the upper hand but chooses not to use it. They restrain themselves because they see a better way. They inherit the earth by changing it. Their character prohibits them from abusing power and is totally opposite of what other powerful people do with their power.

Dr. Jordan Peterson, a University of Toronto professor,

says that the word "meek," as it is used in the Bible, meant people who had weapons, like swords, and had the ability to use them, but were determined to keep them sheathed.[1] In other words, they had the power to pull the sword to control the situation with their power, but they decided that there may be a better outcome if they kept their power under control and their swords sheathed.

Meekness doesn't use its power to retaliate. Meekness has a patience to it. It sees further than the immediate. It realizes power can be displayed to defend, or patience and kindness can keep the sword sheathed with the hope and desire for a better outcome than showing who's the boss and who has the power.

Thank God for the meekness of Jesus. As I am reading what humanity is doing to Him at His trial, I am thinking, Do something, Jesus. Don't let them get away with that. They are wrong and You have the power to stop it. I was saying, "Unsheathe Your sword!"

Matthew says in 27:30–31: **30** "Then they spat on Him,
and took the reed and struck Him on the head. **31** And when
they had mocked Him, they took the robe off Him, put His own clothes on Him, and led Him away to be crucified."

There was mocking, spitting, and hitting before the crucifixion. If there was ever a time to display power, it was then. This was an injustice! But there the Son of Man stood, with a sword that could blow up the earth, and yet it never came out . . . never!

Remember, meekness has a patience to it. It sees further than the immediate. It realizes power can be displayed to defend, or patience and kindness can keep the sword sheathed with the hope and desire for a better outcome than showing who's the boss and who has the power in this situation. Maybe, just maybe, Jesus saw a few hours into the crucifixion story and saw a centurion: a centurion who was probably part of the mocking and part of the charade of mock worship of Jesus in the Praetorium. Instead of wiping out a thousand soldiers in the palace, He knew one would bow at the cross. A centurion, a high-ranking official, would turn from fake worship to real worship. What is amazing is that it did happen.

Matthew 27:54 says, "So when the centurion and those with him, who were guarding Jesus, saw the earthquake and the things that had happened, they feared greatly, saying, 'Truly this was the Son of God!'"

The meekness of Jesus allowed a centurion to come to faith. Displaying meekness by keeping His sword in the sheath would prove to us that meekness not only changed the world, but it started by changing one Roman soldier.

MY PRAYER FOR TODAY

Father, I will find myself with the upper hand at times today. Whether that is in an argument with my children, at the job, or even in my marriage, I am asking for an infusion of meekness. Don't let me have power without meekness. I realize more and more, I need meekness before a promotion. I need meekness with every title and position You grant me. I don't want to be in charge of the earth; I want meekness like our Savior to change the earth, even if it's just one person.

1. Joe Rogan (host) with Jordan Peterson (guest), on *The Joe Rogan Experience*, #1070, January 30, 2018, podcast, 2:28:52, https://www.youtube.com/watch?v=6T7pUEZfgdI.

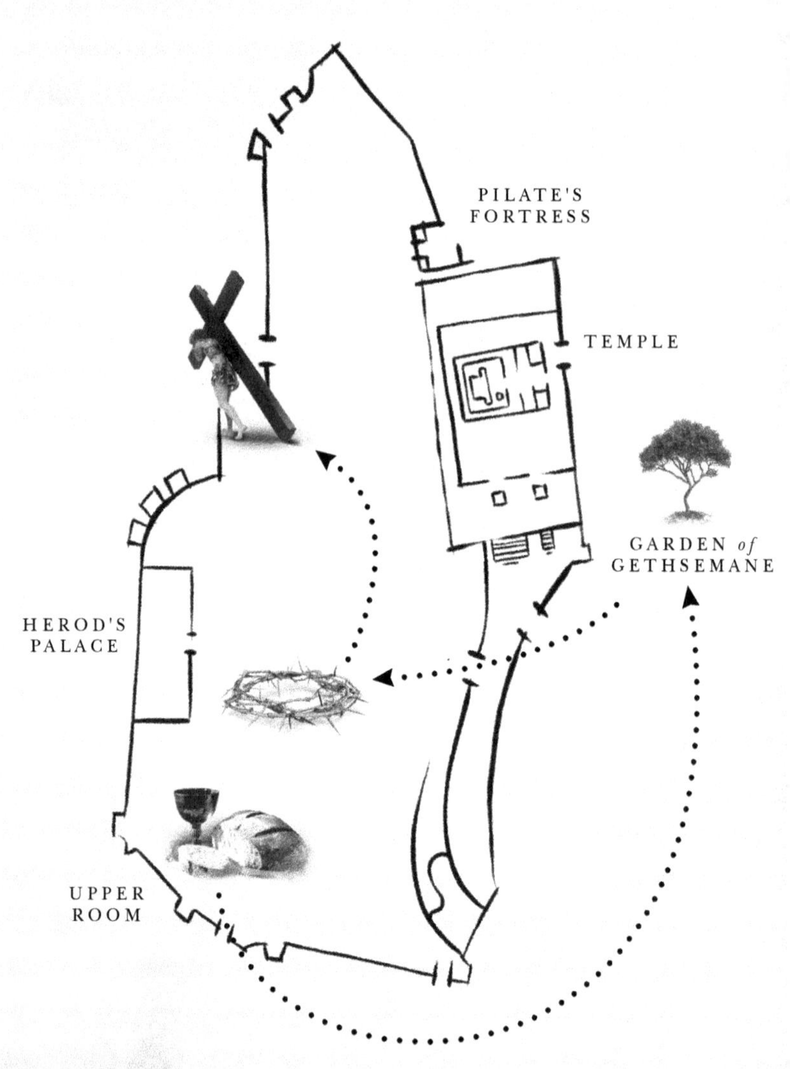
PILATE'S
FORTRESS
TEMPLE
GARDEN of
GETHSEMANE
HEROD'S
PALACE
UPPER
ROOM

PART FOUR

THE WALK

DAY 16

The Half-Mile Walk Has a Name

How far did Jesus have to walk from the Praetorium to Golgotha? How far was it from the trial to His crucifixion site?

When you read the Gospel of John, it simply says in John 19:16–17 (NKJV), "Then he delivered Him to them to be crucified. Then they took Jesus and led Him away. And He, bearing His cross, went out to a place called the Place of a Skull, which is called in Hebrew, Golgotha."

The Roman soldiers led Jesus on a half-mile walk. Many believe it took Jesus one to three hours to walk that half mile. It wasn't the distance that was gruesome, it was a half-mile walk with intense pain.

Church tradition has given a name to this walk of pain. It is called the Via Dolorosa. Via Dolorosa is Latin for the Way of the Sorrows or suffering.[1]

I remember in my teenage years listening to gospel artist Sandi Patty sing the song "Via Dolorosa." It was the first time many Christians realized that the half mile has a name. Church tradition has also marked out fourteen spots on this six-hundred-meter walk. Those spots are called the Stations of the Cross, which indicate places where Jesus paused, spoke to someone, or stumbled.

Though this is only tradition, Christians around the world use those stations to remember the events leading to the crucifixion and death of Jesus by visiting each of the Stations of the Cross. In the city of Jerusalem, the Via Dolorosa is not one street, but a path including several streets, and each of the fourteen stations is indicated with a marker so that sojourners can stop, reflect, and remember the poignancy of these events. Rather than leading outside the city, the final stations in Jerusalem are located in the Church of the Holy Sepulchre, marking the stations of His crucifixion and burial.

The shortness of the Via Dolorosa surprised me. The intensity of the walk overwhelmed me. Because this is what many disciples of Jesus face even today. It's not the distance I am referring to or a place in Jerusalem. Today, we all face a Via Dolorosa. We face pain—sometimes physical, sometimes emotional. It could even be the pain of a child that is off track, yet we still have to walk throughout a day. Our half mile may be just twenty-four hours. We are thinking, I don't know if I can make it through the day. I know of people whose family pain was so severe that they did not know if they would be able to get out of bed.

Jesus' walk reminds me that our Savior made the walk of pain so we can too. He understands what it is to walk with pain.

One of my favorite people to watch lead worship is Southern gospel star TaRanda Greene. We have known TaRanda for almost fifteen years. What has made her one of the greatest worship leaders I know was watching her lead worship while her husband Tony was dying. His kidney was failing, and his future was grim, barring a miracle. We would watch TaRanda take a walk of pain on to stages and platforms and sing to the glory of God. She learned to worship while walking her Via Dolorosa. She was able to do it because Jesus showed us how to walk the half mile. Just when you thought, How can I get up in the morning? Just when you thought, How can I smile? Just when you whispered to yourself, "How can I breathe?"

We are reminded that God's Son's half-mile walk ended at a place called the skull, but that would be the last stop before victory, before a resurrection.

Keep walking, no matter how painful it may seem. Keep walking! God is with you and will give you strength to finish the Via Dolorosa.

MY PRAYER FOR TODAY

Father, it's hard. This is a tough day. My body is in pain, yet I have to smile as I serve my family and go to work. My soul is in pain, as my emotions are running haywire trying to hold on to this marriage. My spirit is in pain, wondering where God is in all of this. Through it all, as the songwriter says, I have learned to trust in Jesus, and I have learned to trust in God. I will make the walk with God's help. I may be in pain, but I am in Christ.

1. "Via dolorosa," *Merriam-Webster.com*, accessed February 11, 2025, https://www.merriam-webster.com/dictionary/via%20dolorosa.

DAY 17

I May Need Help Some Days to Carry My Cross

If Jesus carried the full cross, it is estimated to have weighed around three hundred pounds. Some think that it was only the crossbeam. But even a crossbeam weighs between seventy to one hundred pounds. If you take the higher of the lesser weight, Jesus is carrying one hundred pounds for half a mile. That's hard for even a healthy man to carry. How hard must it have been for a man that has been flogged? Jesus is carrying this weight with his body having undergone the ultimate punishment, flogging.

John 19:1 (NIV) tells us this, "Then Pilate took Jesus and had him flogged." Jesus would walk a half mile with one hundred pounds on his back and having faced the cat o' nine tails.

The Expositors Bible Commentary, commenting on Mark 15:15, said that the Romans would first strip their victims and tie their hands to a post above their head. The whip (flagellum or cat o' nine tails) was made of several pieces of leather with pieces of bone and lead embedded in the ends. The two men who would do the flogging would be on each side of the victim. The Jews limited flogging to a maximum of forty stripes, but the Romans had no such limitation.[1]

The following is a medical description of the physical effects of flogging:

"The heavy whip is brought down with full force again and again across Jesus' shoulders, back, and legs. At first, the heavy thongs cut through the skin only. Then, as the blows continue, they cut deeper in the subcutaneous tissues, producing first an oozing of blood from the capillaries and veins of the skin and finally spurting arterial bleeding from vessels in the underlying muscles. Finally, the skin of the back is hanging in long ribbons, and the entire area is an unrecognizable mass of torn, bleeding tissue."[2]

It is not surprising that victims who faced the flogging of the cat o' nine tails did not survive the beating. Jesus survived, carried His cross, and made the walk to Golgotha.

As Jesus is walking with the cross, He gets unexpected help. Luke 23:26 (NASB) speaks about a miracle on the walk: "And when they led Him away, they laid hold of one Simon of Cyrene, coming in from the country, and placed on him the cross to carry behind Jesus."

A visitor named Simon visits Jerusalem and finds himself right in the middle of the redemption story. Now, Jesus has help to carry His cross.

We are told to carry our cross. There are times I think I will need some help too. I have heavy days where I see there is no way to make it, and out of nowhere, God gives me a Simon.

Jesus told His disciples in Matthew 16:24 (KJV), "If any man will come after me, let him deny himself, and take up his cross, and follow me."

To follow Christ, we will have to take up our cross. What does it mean to take up your cross? "To carry your cross" is a phrase that means to accept and endure personal hardships, difficulties, and sacrifices in order to follow Jesus. It means you are willing to put aside your agenda and desires and commit to God's will first, even when it's hard and painful.

It is much like when Jesus had to carry His physical cross to His crucifixion. It represents a living dedication to Christ regardless the cost, essentially putting your own desires aside and committing to God's will, even when it is challenging or painful. Much like when Jesus carried His physical cross to His crucifixion, it signifies a commitment to self-denial and living a life dedicated to God.

All of us are called to carry our own cross. It will differ for each person. I have watched people carry the cross of a disease, blindness, or being confined to a wheelchair. I have seen the cross of someone married to an unsaved spouse. Your cross could be a geographical location. The place where you live may not welcome Christianity, and you are seen as an enemy, a traitor, and even a disruptor, causing you to worship in secret.

I thank God there are Simons on the hard parts of our journeys. These are the people who were not expected, but somehow they made it into our story. They helped hold a child that I couldn't console. They provided some food when we did not have any. They gave us money when we didn't think we could pay the rent. They drank coffee with us and listened to our story and cried with us.

These are the weight bearers. These are the Simons, and there comes a time on our journey we feel too beat up and too tired to walk and carry our cross, and then, out of nowhere, God sends help.

I take a deep breath and say, "Thank You."

MY PRAYER FOR TODAY

Father, the cross You have asked me to carry is heavy some days. There are moments that I know I am going to collapse under its weight. You see me. You see the weight. I need a weight bearer. I need a strong godly person that can help. God, please send me a Simon. I do pretty well with the walk and the cross, but then there are those days I feel are overwhelming. You did it for Jesus' cross: please do it for mine.

1. Frank E. Gaebelein, D. A. Carson, Walter W. Wessel, and Walter L. Liefeld, *The Expositors Bible Commentary, Volume 8: Matthew, Mark, Luke* (Grand Rapids, MI: 1984), 775–780.

2. C. Truman Davis, "The Crucifixion of Jesus: The Passion of Christ from a Medical Point of View," *Arizona Medicine,* 22, no. 3 (1965): 185.

DAY 18

Why Are There Red Letters Here?

As a pastor, I must tell you that there have been times in my four decades of ministry that someone cornered me after a church service and, with tears in their eyes, poured out their soul to me regardless of the crowd of people around us. I have said on many occasions to such conversations, "This is not the best place for this conversation."

Most of the time, the person accepted it and understood it. They were just so desperate. They just needed help and someone to listen. Most of the time, it was as if they couldn't hold it in any longer and were no longer cognizant of those around them. They frankly didn't care what anyone heard: they needed a sympathetic ear right then.

The oddest place for an important conversation was on the Via Dolorosa. I would have been the first one to say to a group of women and Jesus, "This is just not the best place for this conversation."

Luke 23 gives the most details of the suffering Savior on that half-mile walk than any other gospel. In fact, Luke is the only gospel that puts red letters on the walk.

It's the question I have when I read Luke's account: why are there red letters here? Red letters mean that Jesus is speaking. Many Bibles put the words of Christ in red. Why is Jesus speaking when He is in pain?

We are told about these unique and isolated red letters in Luke 23:26–31 (NKJV):

> **26** Now as they led Him away, they laid hold of a certain
> man, Simon, a Cyrenian, who was coming from the country,
> and on him they laid the cross that he might bear it after
> Jesus. **27** And a great multitude of the people followed Him,
> and women who also mourned and lamented Him. **28** But
> Jesus, turning to them, said, "Daughters of Jerusalem, do
> not weep for Me, but weep for yourselves and for your
> children. **29** For indeed the days are coming in which they
> will say, 'Blessed are the barren, wombs that never bore,
> and breasts which never nursed!' **30** Then they will begin
> to say to the mountains, 'Fall on us!' and to the hills, 'Cover
> us!' **31** For if they do these things in the green wood, what
> will be done in the dry?"

What makes this exchange amazing is how it all began. Jesus answered their tears, not any question or comment. There was a great multitude of people who were at this crucifixion because there was always a crowd at a Jerusalem crucifixion. Something this violent, I believe, would have had more men, but this crucifixion was different. Among the two murderers carrying a cross and making the walk, there was an innocent man sentenced to death who claimed to be the Son of God. We are told from the beginning of Jesus' ministry that women were part of His followers.

What is very evident is that throughout the gospel record, we never read about one woman that came as a skeptic, a cynic, or with a trick question for Jesus. Every one of them who did these things to Jesus was a man. The women of that time knew that Jesus was Who He said He was; that is the reason for all the mourning and the lamenting.

What is interesting is that no man is mourning for Jesus. It is these brave women walking with their broken and beaten Savior, unashamed and courageous to be known as His followers. Their tears were them identifying themselves as believers.

Not only was this an odd place for the red letters of Jesus, but to the casual eye, the topic seems to be out of place. The women are weeping for the Jesus on His way to the cross, and Jesus is pointing them to a prophetic event decades into the future. Jesus is speaking about what He said in Luke 19 (that Jerusalem is going to experience a destruction in the near future). Jesus was telling these women that it will be hard for them when Jerusalem is attacked. He is saying this with a cross on His back and bleeding profusely.

Jesus is thinking of others and not Himself because Jesus always thinks of others and not Himself. As an example, the teachings of Jesus and the miracles of Jesus always elevated and dignified the women of the first century. While tradition and laws tried to define women as objects, Jesus gave them an identity, and He did it all the way to the cross. He was preparing them for their difficult future. Rome would come and destroy Jerusalem in 70 AD, and Jesus is thinking of their future pain instead of His pain that is just a few meters away.

How do people think of others' pain when they themselves are in agony? Those are the places of the unusual red letters. It's the place where you should be worried about your future, and somehow you are worried about those around you.

This is the mark of a man or woman who has taken up their cross. God somehow gives them an ability to look beyond themselves and find a way to be a help to others.

They are willing to overlook their needs. They are willing to overlook their pain. They are willing to overlook their grim future to make someone else's future better. That is Jesus speaking to grieving women with a three-hundred-pound cross on His back. He is willing to stop and help them when He is the One who needs help.

My present pain doesn't prohibit me from speaking to another's pain if I am daily carrying my cross.

MY PRAYER FOR TODAY

Father, there are so many days of grief and pain that I have experienced, but I think I have experienced them selfishly. Please forgive me, because even though I am in pain, it doesn't preclude me from carrying my cross. I carry my cross on sunny days and dark days. Help me on the dark days to speak words of life to others when my flesh wants me to pay more attention to it than those who are crying in my presence. Help me to stop. Help me to have those odd red-letter days for others.

DAY 19

There Were Multitudes but Not a Lot of Family

It's important for people to know if you are in the multitudes or in the family. As Jesus is walking from His trial to the hill called Calvary, we see two groups of people who are witnesses to this man's death. Though Jesus will die for every man and woman in the world, there is a distinction that is made by Luke.

We read in Luke 23:27–28 (NKJV): **27** "And a great multitude of the people followed Him, and women who also mourned and lamented Him. **28** But Jesus, turning to them, said, 'Daughters of Jerusalem, . . .'"

There is a great multitude, and there are crying women He will call daughters. The difference is epic. The grouping is critical to identify because every man must decide what this dying Jesus is to them.

I can't get away from the words that "a great multitude followed Him." But this is not the same "followed Him" as what happened to the twelve disciples.

From the beginning of Jesus' ministry, the words "follow Me" was His calling card for a life of discipleship and eventually to change the world. When Jesus started His public ministry, He would say "follow Me." Men would leave everything, as scripture tells us "and followed Him."

Matthew 4:18–22 (NASB) shows us how important these words were from the get-go:

> **18** And walking by the Sea of Galilee, He saw two
> brothers, Simon who was called Peter, and Andrew
> his brother, casting a net into the sea; for they were
> fishermen. **19** And He *said to them, "Follow Me,
> and I will make you fishers of men." **20** And they
> immediately left the nets, and followed Him. **21** And
> going on from there He saw two other brothers,
> James the son of Zebedee, and John his brother, in
> the boat with Zebedee their father, mending their
> nets; and He called them. **22** And they immediately
> left the boat and their father, and followed Him.

He would call them and they would follow.

One thing to remember, it was never "multitudes" that would "follow Him." They would hear Jesus. They would be recipients of His miracles, but that doesn't mean they followed Jesus. On that day, He walked the road of suffering, the multitudes followed Him, but they did not follow Him. They wanted to see another Jesus show, but they were not committed to Jesus' Lordship. To follow Jesus was to believe in Jesus. To follow Jesus was to live for Jesus. To follow Jesus was to have everything change.

I believe it was critical that Jesus spoke to the women in front of the following multitudes. When Jesus addressed the mourning women, He called them daughters.

This is significant. He was speaking to them as part of His family. He was not speaking to the following multitudes but to the crying ladies.

People confuse God as their Father when they must

remember that God is their Creator first. God created the heavens and the earth. God gave us life. God gives us blessing every day. But those things don't automatically translate to God being my Father.

Though I may start the Lord's prayer with "Our Father," we may have a startling realization that I am saying "Our Father" when, in actuality, God is not. For Him to be Father, a decision has to be made on our part.

Jesus went to the cross to redeem His creation. He went to Calvary to give every person on the planet an opportunity to leave the multitudes and enter into the family of God. We all must decide someday where we stand. Do we stand in the crowd with the multitudes that observe, listen, and receive? Or do we stand with the sons and daughters that made God our Father?

In my case, there was an adoption that took place. There came a moment that I asked God to forgive me of my sins and take me in as one of His own.

When Jesus distinguished family from the multitudes, He did it on the path to the cross. He was telling us that this will be and will forever be the path to adoption into the family of God.

MY PRAYER FOR TODAY

Father, I thank You that I can call You "Father." Help me not to take it for granted. Jesus spilled His blood and suffered unimaginable pain so that I can call You "Father." I thank You that You adopted me. I thank You that You did not reject me. Many multitudes are in a religion but have never experienced adoption by God. Thank You, Father, that You are still adopting people every day. No one is refused who wants to be Your son and daughter.

DAY 20

It's Hard Enough Lord, I Don't Think I Can Handle Another Thing

Many times, when I am going through a hard season in my life, I am looking for the leading of the Holy Spirit for next steps. I have always defined next steps as the way out of this hard place I am presently in. I am waiting on God to show me the exit door from this season.

But what happens when you feel the guidance of the Holy Spirit, and you sense it's the end of this hard chapter, only to open the exit door and discover that it's "hard season number two" waiting for you? I would be thinking, It's hard enough Lord, I don't think I can handle another thing.

Jesus goes from a betrayal by Judas to His disciples sleeping on Him when they should have been praying for Him. Then comes the arrest and quick movement to the mock trial of Jesus with false accusers speaking lies about Him.

After the Roman soldiers scourge Him and the Jewish people cry, "Crucify Him," they take Jesus on a walk which has in its view a place they call the skull, Golgotha. John 19:16–17 (NKJV) says, **16** "Then he delivered Him to them to be crucified. Then they took Jesus and led Him away. **17** And He, bearing His cross, went out to a place called the Place of a Skull, which is called in Hebrew, Golgotha."

It seemed for the Son of God that every exit door that Jesus opened was an entrance door into another point of pain.

What do you do when you thought you were coming out of something painful and you find you are actually coming into another difficult season? Welcome to the hardest twenty-four hours any human has ever faced. Welcome to the day Jesus was going to the cross.

For Him, every door was another door into suffering. Jesus could see His next chapter coming from Via Dolorosa because Golgotha was a hill. It was an elevated place known for thousands of deaths. Golgotha wasn't the crucifixion site of Jesus and two murderers. Golgotha was the execution site of many people. During times of war and rebellion, hundreds or even thousands of people were crucified in a short period of time by the Romans. During the siege of Jerusalem in 70 AD, Roman troops crucified up to five hundred Jews per day for several months. That place is known for killing, and its ground has soaked up much blood.

Because Golgotha was a hill, it allowed many bystanders to witness death from a distance. Because the crucifixion of Jesus was during Passover week, some believe thousands watched the crucifixion of Jesus. The city knew that when someone was being walked down a certain road and up a certain hill, this meant the end. Not only did the public know what was going to happen, but, more importantly, Jesus also knew what was about to happen.

He knew the final chapter in this pain saga was in front of Him. He could see the hill. He could see the gathering of the masses to watch His crucifixion. Jesus saw Golgotha from a distance and knew because Scripture had already prophesied it. Jesus knew that there would be multiple doors of pain awaiting Him. Psalm 22 predicted His feet and hands would be pierced, and His bones would not be broken. Jesus knew that underneath Him, men would gamble for His clothing. And Jesus also knew that He would be mocked and verbally abused.

Isaiah 53 would give the bigger picture that this pain was not in vain but that the sins of the world would be laid on Him. Jesus knew all of this because He is the Author of what was written about this moment. This moment was no surprise: every way out of one pain led to more pain, and the final place would be ultimate pain on that hill.

I have to believe that this is the hard part for every Christian on the cross walk. We have this notion that life is good and great, and then a tough time comes. God leads us out and we are back to the good season. God would never take us into back-to-back-to-back pain seasons . . . or would He?

I think this walk of Jesus prepares us for these kinds of moments. Jesus tells us in Matthew 10:24 (ESV), "A disciple is not above his teacher," so don't expect to audit this class. I have listened to stories when a child is taking care of a senior-citizen parent who then takes a turn for the worse from an illness or disease. Then it goes from companionship to intense care. Then, the compassionate child realizes that Mom doesn't have money for the nursing care she so desperately needs, and that she (the daughter) still has to work her job to provide for her own family. She realizes that her own family is barely making ends meet, and now she is adding her mom's expenses. The daughter is now faced with issues of finances and exhaustion. Then she opens up another door and starts to process the deterioration of a parent who loves her and what it would be like when they die. And she soon finds herself changing the diapers of the elderly parent who changed her diapers as a child.

It's a season of back-to-back-to-back hardship. And even if she could see ahead, it looks like a skull and more pain.

Perhaps you've been in this season (or something similar to it) yourself.

But be of good courage. Jesus took this walk before. He understands it. You can rejoice because though many doors seem like an entrance into more pain, there is coming a door that is actually one into a tomb that will bring victory and resurrection. Hold on tight: it may be tough, but there will be life at the end of what seems to be nothing but death for the future. It may be hard, but He will give you the strength and wisdom you need.

MY PRAYER FOR TODAY

Father, just when I thought I was done with this difficulty, another awaits me. I thought this last thing I went through depleted me of all strength. And then I remember, You are my strength. I have You inside of me. Just when I think I can't do this any longer, I remember Who lives inside of me and gives me everything I need to face another day, even if that next day still holds more challenges. I am confident of this one thing: You are with me, and You will see me through.

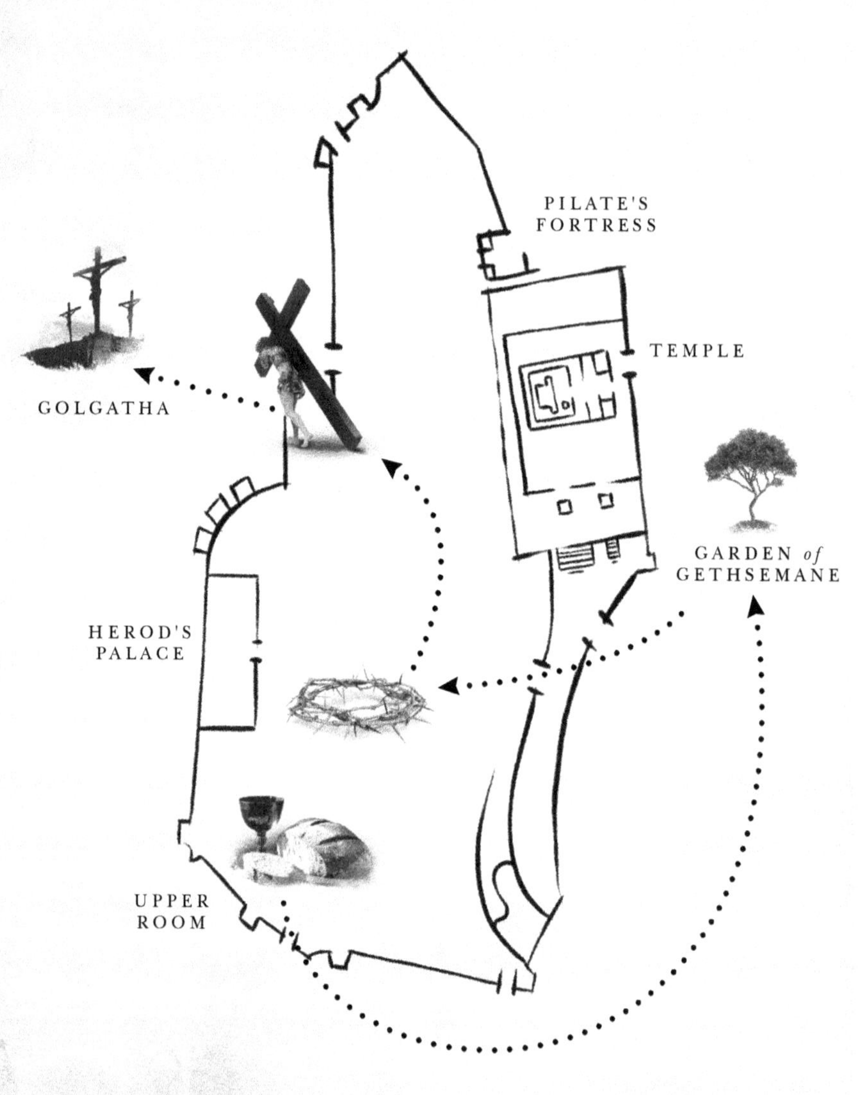
PILATE'S
FORTRESS
TEMPLE
GOLGATHA
GARDEN of
GETHSEMANE
HEROD'S
PALACE
UPPER
ROOM

PART FIVE

THE CROSS

DAY 21

One Word for Three Worlds

There have been iconic words that have been spoken through the course of human history that have gotten into the fabric of our society and have been etched on our minds so firmly that we can finish the sentences.

They have lived with us for decades. and from Hollywood to history, we can finish them. There are fun phrases like, "Toto, I've a feeling we are not in Kansas anymore"[1] and "I'm going to make him an offer he can't refuse."[2] We remember the Austrian accent of "I'll be back"[3] and the English accent of "[My name is] Bond, James Bond."[4]

History has given us, "Give me liberty or give me death"[5] and "Ask not what your country can do for you but what you can do for your country."[6] We remember these words from two assassinated presidents: "We have nothing to fear but fear itself"[7] and "Four score and seven years ago."[8]

When man tried to go to the moon and ran into problems we heard, "Houston, we've had a problem."[9] And when man finally landed on the moon we heard, "One small step for man . . . one giant leap for mankind."[10]

And who can forget the words "I have a dream?"[11]

There is one phrase that ascends head and shoulders

above them all. Only one phrase goes deeper, further, and wider. Its impact is as high as the heavens and as low as the bowels of hell. It was a cry and a dying man's final words.

In John 19:30 (NIV), "Jesus said, 'It is finished.' With that, He bowed His head and gave up His spirit."

"It is finished" was the cry of a dying man but not just any man: These were the final words of the Son of Man and the Son of God on the cross. It happened on the day we call Good Friday.

Take note of two important things when He uttered those words from the cross. Jesus did not say, "I am finished" but "It is finished." The emphasis is on the two-letter word "it."

That small two-letter word was a global assignment. It was why He died on that cross.

The assignment is explicitly expressed in Matthew 20:28: "just as the Son of Man did not come to be served, but to serve, and to give his life as a ransom for many." Ransom was the price paid for those held in captivity, and Jesus' death paid it. All of humanity is released from the captivity of sin.

Most importantly, "It is finished" is one word in the Greek language. The New Testament, which was written in Greek, has it as one word! It is the Greek word "tetelestai."

When a person in the first century incurred a debt that they could not pay, the person to whom they owed it would write out their debt, listing how much they owed, and they would nail that on the doorpost of the debtor's house so that everyone who walked by would know that they were in debt.

Can you imagine your Visa or Amex bill nailed to the front of your home so everyone can know you are in debt? That was the custom.

But there was another custom. If that bill was paid in full, something else would be public. They would write the word "tetelestai" on business documents, indicating that a bill had been paid in full. When those three nails were driven through Jesus, it meant humanity's debt was paid in full. The debt is finished—tetelestai.

When Jesus uttered those words from the cross, it was one word for three worlds. He was speaking to heaven, hell, and earth. Heaven rejoiced and got ready. Hell shuddered in disbelief, and earth was overwhelmed by love that someone would pay their debt.

Tetelestai was one word for three worlds. When heaven heard the pounding of the nails, it meant, "Get ready: a lot of people are on their way up here." Jesus' death is the acceptable payment for this to happen.

When hell started to hear the pounding of the nails, hell realized it had lost what it had thought it controlled: death.

John tells us in Revelation 1:18 (KJV), "I am he that liveth, and was dead; and, behold, I am alive for evermore, Amen; and have the keys of hell and of death."

Max Lucado said, "On the eve of the cross, Jesus made his decision. He would rather go to hell for you than go to heaven without you."[12]

Tetelestai meant hand over control, hand over the keys.

Finally, when earth heard the pounding of the nails, earth was overwhelmed by love that someone would pay their debt.

If you have ever wondered if God loves you, just look at the cross. Remember the words of John 3:16 (NASB):

"For God so loved the world, that He gave His only Son so that everyone who believes in Him will not perish, but have eternal life."

Our debt is paid in full.

1. "Toto, I've a feeling we're not in Kansas anymore," from *The Wizard of Oz*, directed by Victor Fleming (1939; Culver City, CA: Metro-Goldwyn-Mayer), DVD.

2. "I'm going to make him an offer he can't refuse," from *The Godfather*, directed by Francis Ford Coppola (1972; Hollywood, CA: Paramount Pictures), DVD.

3. "I'll be back," from *Terminator 2: Judgment Day*, directed by James Cameron (1991; Hollywood, CA: Paramount Pictures), DVD.

4. "[The name is] Bond, James Bond," first said in *Dr. No*, directed by Terence Young (1962; London: Eon Productions), DVD.

5. "Give me liberty or give me death," Patrick Henry, Speech to the Second Virginia Convention, March 23, 1775.

6. "Ask not what your country can do for you but what you can do for your country," President John F. Kennedy in his inaugural address on January 20, 1961.

MY PRAYER FOR TODAY

Father, all I can say is thank You. My sin debt has been paid. You truly died the death I was supposed to die. You lived the life I could not live, and You gave me a reward I don't deserve. I take this day to say thank You, Father, for sending Your Son to pay the price.

I have been set free.

7. "We have nothing to fear but fear itself," President Franklin D. Roosevelt in his first inaugural address on March 4, 1933.

8. "Four score and seven years ago" is a quote from President Abraham Lincoln's Gettysburg Address, which he gave on November 19, 1863.

9. John Uri, Johnson Space Center, "50 Years Ago: Houston, We've Had a Problem," Nasa.gov, https://www.nasa.gov/history/50-years-ago-houston-weve-had-a-problem/.

10. "One small step for man . . . one giant leap for mankind" were words spoken by astronaut Neil Armstrong when he first stepped onto the moon on July 20, 1969, after Apollo 11 landed.

11. "I have a dream," words from Martin Luther King's "I Have a Dream" speech, Washington, DC, August 28, 1963.

12. Max Lucado, God So Loved You: *A 40-Day Devotional for Spiritual Growth* (Nashville: Thomas Nelson, 2007), Kindle.

DAY 22

Someone Paid Our Bill, and We Did the Damage

This really happened to my family at a Texas Roadhouse restaurant.

As we were finishing our meal, I noticed that the waitress brought our check, then took it away, and then brought it back again. She placed it on the table, and then smiled and said, “Somebody in the restaurant paid for your meal. You're all set.”

And then she walked away.

I had the strangest feeling sitting there. The feeling was helplessness. There was nothing I could do. It had been taken care of. To insist on paying would have been pointless.

All I could do was trust that what she said was actually true and then live in that—which meant getting up and leaving the restaurant. My acceptance of what she said gave me a choice: to live like it was true or to create my own reality in which the bill was not paid. It was so hard to reconcile that we did the damage, we ate the food (a lot of food), and yet we were the recipients of the generosity of someone else. To actually trust that we don’t owe anything is incredible.

That was a good day, and that is why we call the day of the cross Good Friday. It was a good day for humanity. For it was on this day that someone paid the bill for every person on the planet.

Seven hundred years before the cross happened, Isaiah the prophet explained why it's good. Isaiah 53:5 (NKJV) says, "But He was wounded for our transgressions, He was bruised for our iniquities; The chastisement for our peace was upon Him, And by His stripes we are healed."

The key word in Isaiah 53 is "our," not "His," but "our." Who crucified Jesus that day? I did and you did. It was not the Romans. It was not Pilate. It was not the Jews. All of us are responsible.

I remember the words of John R. W. Stott when he said, "Before we can begin to see the cross as something done for us, . . . we have to see it as something done by us. . . ."[1]

Jesus was punished for my sin because sin had to be punished! If my sin was not transferred to Jesus, then someone still had to pay for it because sin is a crime against God. All crimes must be paid for. You and I would not be here if we had to pay for it. Someone had to die for committing crimes against God. It was Jesus. Jesus died, but the amazing thing is that the one who died rose again. Jesus' death is the acceptable payment.

The apostle Paul said in Romans 5:10 (NASB), "We were reconciled to God by the death of His Son." In Romans 5:1, he also said, "We have peace with God through Jesus Christ."

All this means is that you can't leave Jesus out of the equation if you want to have a relationship with God. To make friends with God, it's not by your promises or good deeds but through Jesus. Jesus died so we would not have to. Jesus died so we might live.

Friday is a good Friday. In fact, Friday is a great Friday for all of humanity. Our bill was being paid that day.

There was an old comic strip some years ago called B.C. It was called that because it was set back in the cavemen days, way back in BC. Though it was about prehistoric people, the content of their conversations was anything but.

My favorite B.C. comic was two cavemen speaking about the death of Christ. One Neanderthal said, "I hate the term 'Good Friday.'" His friend asked why. "My Lord was hung on a tree that day," the Neanderthal replied.

The friend then asked, "If you were going to be hanged on that day and He volunteered to take your place, how would you feel?" The man said, "Good!"

As the friend walked away from the conversation, he said, "Have a nice day."[2]

Someone summed it up like this, "It's Good Friday because two thousand years ago, the events of today prove that we matter to God."

We did the damage, and He paid our bill.

MY PRAYER FOR TODAY

Father, I am overwhelmed that You pay my bill for me. You would pay the price with Your own life. I don't think I can say "thank You" better than the lyrics of Horatio Spafford's second verse of "It Is Well": "My sin, oh the bliss of this glorious thought. My sin, not in part but the whole. Was nailed to the cross and I bear it no more. Praise the Lord, Praise the Lord, Oh my soul."[3]

1. John Stott, Dale Larsen, and Sandy Larsen, *The Cross of Christ*, 20th Anniversary ed. (Lisle, IL: Intervarsity Press, 2006), 15.

2. Johnny Hart, "B.C. Comic Strip," Facebook, "A favorite 'Johnny' Good Friday strip from 2001 . . ." March 30, 2018, https://www.facebook.com/BCcomic/posts/a-favorite-johnny-good-friday-strip-from-2001/10151092037974978/.

3. Sankey, Ira David, *My Life and the Story of the Gospel Hymns* (New York: Harper & Brothers, 1906), 168-70.

DAY 23

Twice Mine

One of my favorite stories is the one of a father and son who worked for months to build a toy sailboat.

Every night, when he came home from work, the man and his boy would disappear into the garage for hours. It was a labor of love—love for each other and for the thing they were creating. The wooden hull was painted bright red, and it was trimmed with gleaming white sails.

When it was finished, they traveled to a nearby lake for the boat's trial run. Before launching it, the father tied a string to its stern to keep it from sailing too far. The boat performed beautifully, but before long, a motorboat crossing the lake cut the string, and the sailboat drifted out of sight on the large lake. Attempts to find it were fruitless, and both father and son wept over its loss.

A few weeks later as the boy was walking home from school, he passed a secondhand store and was amazed to see a toy sailboat in the window—his sailboat! He ran inside to claim the boat, telling the proprietor about his experience on the lake. The store owner explained that he had found the boat while on a fishing trip.

"You may be its maker," he said, "but as a finder, I am its legal owner. You may have it back—for fifty dollars."

The boy was stunned at how much it would cost him to regain his boat, but since it was so precious to him, he quickly set about earning the money to buy it back. Months later, he joyfully walked into the toy store and handed the owner fifty dollars in exchange for his sailboat.

It was the happiest day of his life. As he left the store, he held the boat up to the sunlight. Its colors gleamed as though newly painted.

"I made you, but I lost you," he said. "Now I've bought you back. That makes you twice mine, and twice mine is mine forever."

Twice mine resonates in my soul as what God has done for us. He created us, but He has purchased us on the cross.

Calvary was a transactional moment between God the Son and God the Father. The Creator of man saw man lost by man's own free will in Genesis 3. Man chose sin and not God. And through thousands of years, sinful man has been wandering trying to find his way back home to God. What man did not realize is that he can't find God: it's the other way around. God finds him.

The whole Bible can be summed up as the condition of sinful man and the rescue plan of a loving God. The rescue plan culminated in this transaction on the cross . . . what was happening when God put all the sin of the world and laid it on His Son.

This was that fifty-dollar moment for the boat. This was buying back that which was lost. It wasn't a speedboat that cut the tie, but sin cut the tie between God and man. The transaction is so well paraphrased through Eugene Peterson's Message (MSG) version of the Bible when he says in 2 Corinthians 5:19, "God put the world square with himself through the Messiah, giving the world a fresh start by offering forgiveness of sins. God has given us the task of telling everyone what he is doing."

And what is God doing? Peterson paraphrases verse 20: "We're Christ's representatives. God uses us to persuade men and women to drop their differences and enter into God's work of making things right between them. We're speaking for Christ himself now: Become friends with God; he's already a friend with you."

We can be friends with God because of the cross. We have been purchased after we were created.

The eighteenth-century pastor/hymnwriter Philip Doddridge wrote the hymn called "O Happy Day." Speaking of Calvary, the lyrics say, "Tis done! The great transaction's done! I am my Lord's and He is mine; He drew me, and I followed on; Charmed to confess the voice divine."[1]

The great transaction completed on a hill called the skull. My debt was paid. But this transaction revealed much more. For the Son of God to give His life for me, heaven was making an epic statement. As Erwin Lutzer said, "If the value of an article is dependent upon the price paid for it, then Christ's death made our value skyrocket. Let no one say we are worthless. God is not a foolish investor; He would never invest in that which is worthless."[2]

The cross says you are valuable enough to God for Him to give His Son's life.

MY PRAYER FOR TODAY

Father, I am overwhelmed that You would give Your Son for me. I am stirred with the thought of this kind of sacrifice. Whenever voices get in my head that scream, "worthless, useless, and defective," I will remember the cross. For it was there You said that by the death of Your Son, I am valuable to You.

1. "Oh Happy Day, That Fixed My Choice," accessed February 17, 2025, HymnTime, http://www.hymntime.com/tch/htm/o/h/a/p/ohappdad.htm.

2. Erwin Lutzer, as quoted in "Fix Your Eyes," accessed February 26, 2025, https://storage.cloversites.com/lemmc/documents/Fix%20Your%20Eyes.pdf.

DAY 24

The Question of the Ages

The Bible is filled with immense questions. Cain wondered, "Am I my brother's keeper?" Moses asked, "Who is on the Lord's side?" Job, in his suffering, said, "If a man die, shall he live again?" David, at a weak moment, asked, "What is man that Thou art mindful of him?" Malachi asked the people of God, "Will a man rob God?" A Philippian jailor who witnessed a miracle happen asked, "What must I do to be saved?"

There is one question that stands above them all. It's a question for humanity that was posed by a governor.

Pilate has Jesus next to him, a crowd in front of him, and he asks this question in Matthew 27:22 (NASB): "Pilate *said to them, 'Then what shall I do with Jesus who is called Christ?'"

What makes this somewhat chilling is where the gospel writer says Pilate asked it from. Matthew 27:19 says, "While he was sitting on the judgment seat."

The judgment seat: Pilate? Seriously? How ironic and humorous at the same time to see a man judging the Son of Man. Pilate has no idea that he will be judged as to his answer of what to do with Jesus.

Pilate's question also had Pilate's conflict. He tried every way he could to evade the only answer to the question, "What shall I do with Jesus?" To answer that question correctly would cost him everything.

His wife had a disturbing dream the night before this epic question and was really trying to help her husband. She called Jesus a righteous man. It seemed every way Pilate tried to avoid the real answer just made things more complicated. What shall I do with Jesus? The right answer is fall at His feet and worship Him. That was not going to happen that night in the Praetorium.

When Pilate faced this question, he evaded it in five ways.

First, he tried reason. He said, "I find no fault in Him." He tried to reason with logic and not accept the conflict of his heart that was challenging him to go beyond the crowd.

Reason would always be challenged and squashed by the chanting, "Crucify Him! Crucify Him!" The shouts silenced his logical reason.

Second, Pilate also sought to turn Him over to someone else. He would let others make the decision for him. He wanted to send Jesus back to Herod. In disgust, Herod sent Him back to Pilate. When the dust settled, Jesus was still in Pilate's hands, and the question was still unanswered.

A third way Pilate sought to avoid bowing his knees in surrender was in a quest to find a compromise. He tried to scourge Him and let Him go. He thought that should be enough to quell the shouts.

That night, the crowd wanted a crucifixion. That night, Jesus would die. The only question still on the table is if Pilate would surrender to his conscience and conviction.

Pilate even tried to substitute somebody else. He tried to let go of Barabbas, a murderer, and release Jesus for a worse man. Pilate was wanting to make Barabbas a substitute when the real Substitute was next to him.

Finally, Pilate tried to proclaim himself clean by washing his hands in water. Pilate tried to figure out another way of cleansing his conscience.

Men do that all over the world and throughout the ages. We will try cleansing our guilty consciences by doing good things. We will say, "I am a good person." We will say, "I have not hurt anyone" and "I love everybody." Those are all handwashing methods to avoid the question, "What will you do with Jesus?"

The cross exposes the true nature and character of the world. We will avoid the question of the ages and come up with our own answers and ways. The cross is a rebuke to the human race, who make up answers instead of wanting the truth.

All other religions, with no exception, teach that heaven, the afterlife, or whatever name they call it, is what we get as a result of our good works. Christianity is the only religion in the world that promises we get to heaven as a result of what God does for us, not what we do for God. Martin Luther convicts us all when he said, "What makes you think that God is more pleased with your good deeds than He is with His blessed Son?"[1]

For many years, I have asked crowds of people this question: "How do you get to heaven?" In every room, there are hundreds of different answers. And I will express every time how all these different answers perplex me. We have people in the room that are so sure of how to get to heaven, yet they have never been there. They seem to have come up with directions to a place they have never experienced.

So why not listen to the One Who has been there? Only Jesus truly knows that answer.

We will never surrender our directions for His if we don't answer the question correctly: "What will I do with Jesus?" This is the question of the ages and the question of your life.

Here is the answer: fall at His feet and declare He is God and that He is the only way. That is the only answer that will change your forever.

MY PRAYER FOR TODAY

Father, I can answer the question of the ages for myself. "What shall I do with Jesus?" I will call Him Lord. I will call Him King. I will call Him Savior. I will fall at His feet and submit to Him. No diversions, no excuses, and no distractions: I must come face to face with Christ.

1. Adolph Spaeth, L.D. Reed, Henry Eyster Jacobs, et al., trans. & eds., *Works of Martin Luther* (Philadelphia: A. J. Holman Company, 1915), Vol. 1, 173-285. See also "A Treatise on Good Works by Dr. Martin Luther, 1520, (a selection)," https://www.bluffton.edu/courses/tlc/nislyl/hum2/luther.htm.

DAY 25

His Pain Became My Gain

If Peter the apostle had his way, there would have been no cross. And if there was no cross, there would have been no resurrection. Hell would have been victorious. Redemption of the world would have been thwarted.

Peter tried to stop Jesus from going to the cross. When Jesus began to tell his disciples about His suffering, Peter did one of the most arrogant things of his three-year disciple career. He tried to stop Jesus from dying for the world.

The Gospel of Matthew gives us the exchange in 16:21–22 (NLT):

> **21** From then on Jesus began to tell his disciples plainly that it was necessary for him to go to Jerusalem, and that he would suffer many terrible things at the hands of the elders, the leading priests, and the teachers of religious law. He would be killed, but on the third day he would be raised from the dead.
> **22** But Peter took him aside and began to reprimand him for saying such things. "Heaven forbid, Lord," he said. "This will never happen to you!"

Jesus turns to Peter and gives him the harshest rebuke found in the Gospels. He tells Peter in Matthew 16:23, "Get behind me, Satan."

Jesus is talking to Peter but says Satan. Was Jesus calling Peter Satan? I don't think so. I think Jesus was addressing hell with Peter in front of him. Peter was not the devil, but his words were from the pit of hell.

The disciple who tried to stop the cross would write profoundly about the cross. Peter's revelation of calvary is powerful. He tells us in 1 Peter 2:24 (TLB) what was happening on the day he tried to prevent. Peter writes, "He personally carried the load of our sins in his own body when he died on the cross so that we can be finished with sin and live a good life from now on. For his wounds have healed ours!"

What a thought! What a statement! Jesus would personally carry our load of sins so that we can be finished with the curse and the weight of sin and live a victorious life. In essence, His pain became our gain!

When Peter said, "He personally carried the load of our sins," he was eating his own words about Jesus not going to the cross. So effectively did he learn his lesson that six times over in this letter he refers to the suffering of Christ.

Peter eventually got it because Peter needed the cross. He realized that people in the world mattered so much to God that He would put His own Son in their place to die for them so that guilty parties like you and me (and Peter), such undeserving people, could go free. In other words, our sins were transferred to Christ. It was our sins that He bore, says Peter, because in the verse before, verse 22, Peter tells us: "He committed no sin."

So those sins were my sins. Those sins He carried were your sins. Those sins He bore were Peter's sins.

Peter, a Jew who had been brought up under the old dispensation, knew what it was to bring a lamb to the priest to make atonement for his sin. He had known what it was to lay his hand upon the head of that animal, transferring his own sin to the lamb. He had known what it was to see that animal's blood being shed for his sin.

What Peter was saying, in effect, was that when Christ came, He Himself was the Lamb of God that takes away the sin of the world. He would be the great sacrifice for the whole world.

Peter's words describe what happens now in our lives. Our sins have been forgiven, and we can live the life God intended us to live.

The blessing of Calvary continues. Peter tells us more in 1 Peter 3:18 (NKJV): "For Christ also suffered once for sins, the just for the unjust, that He might bring us to God. . . ."

The death of Christ is to get us to God. And Jesus proved it immediately on Calvary.

As He died between two thieves, one of them would realize that the man dying next to Him was the One that can bring him to God. Luke tells us in 23:43 (TLB) that Jesus would promise this: "And Jesus replied, 'Today you will be with me in Paradise. This is a solemn promise.'"

Calvary must happen for man to be promised heaven. What a promise we have. He would die the death I was supposed to die so that I might live the life He wanted me to live. Matthew Henry said:

> When Christ died He left a will in which He gave His soul to His Father, His body to Joseph of Arimathea, His clothes to the soldiers, and His

mother to John. But to His disciples, who had left all to follow Him, He left not silver or gold, but something far better—Heaven![1]

Calvary gets us to God. Calvary opens up the gates of heaven. His pain was my gain.

MY PRAYER FOR TODAY

Father, thank You for the gift of Your Son. I can say with assurance that because of His sacrifice for me, I have gained eternity. His pain was my gain. I have gained a relationship with God. I have gained the forgiveness of God, and I have gained all the promises of God. Thank You, Jesus, for not listening to Peter.

1. Matthew Henry and Leslie F. Church, *The NIV Matthew Henry Commentary in One Volume: Based on the Broad Oak Edition* (New York: Harper Collins, 1992), 5866.

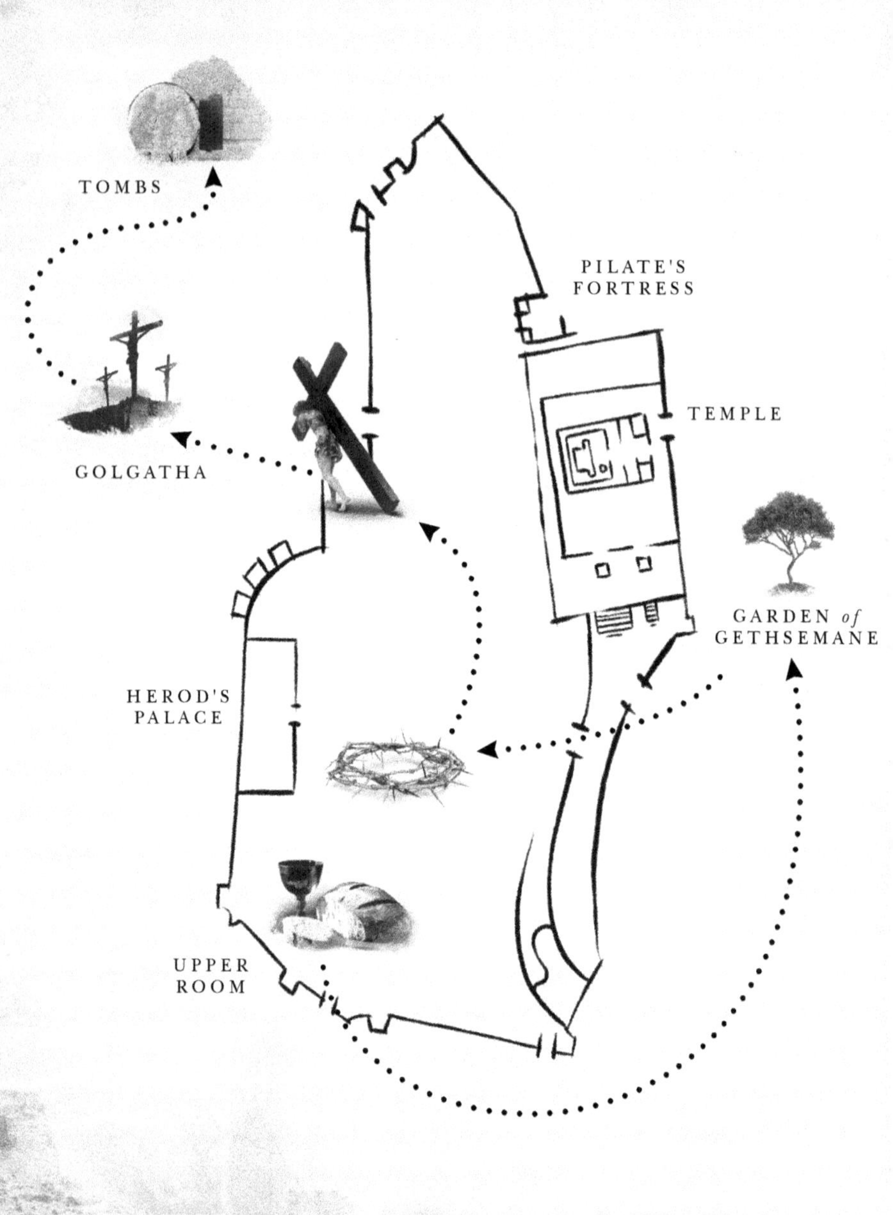
TOMBS
PILATE'S
FORTRESS
TEMPLE
GOLGATHA
GARDEN of
GETHSEMANE
HEROD'S
PALACE
UPPER
ROOM

PART SIX

THE GRAVE

DAY 26

What Does Easter Really Mean?

I heard the story about a group of four-year-olds who were gathered in a Sunday school class in Chattanooga, Tennessee. Their enthusiastic teacher looked at the class and asked this question: "Does anyone know what today is?"

A little four-year-old girl, Becky, held up her finger and said, "Yes, today is Easter."

The teacher exclaimed, "That's fantastic! Now, does anyone know what makes it Easter?"

The same little girl responded and said, "Yes, it is Easter because Jesus rose from the grave."

But before the teacher could congratulate her, she continued, "But if he sees his shadow, he has to go back in for seven weeks."

Obviously, this girl mixed up Jesus and a groundhog.

Believe it or not, there are people still that get mixed up about this day. We don't know if we are dealing with Easter Jesus or the Easter Bunny! Is Easter about chocolate, peeps, and egg hunts? Or is Easter about something more?

Jon Stewart, news pundit, satirist, and host of *The Daily Show* wasn't off the mark when he said,

> A guy comes down to earth, takes your sins, dies, and comes back three days later. You believe in him and go to heaven forever. How do you get from that to hide the eggs? Did Jesus have a problem with eggs? Did he go, "When I come back, if I see any eggs, the whole salvation thing is off."[1]

Though there is humor in this, there is also truth in what Stewart said. The resurrection is the exclamation point on the mission of heaven being accomplished. It does not stop at the cross but at His resurrection.

Easter tells us that death doesn't win. God wins! Historian Arnold Toynbee said, "Find the body of that Jew, and Christianity crumbles into ruins."[2]

The good news is, you can't find it unless you go to heaven.

On one occasion, Michelangelo, the great artist, turned on his fellow artists in a spirit of indignation. He said:

> Why do you keep filling gallery after gallery with endless pictures on the one theme of Christ in weakness, Christ on the Cross, and most of all, Christ hanging dead? Why do you concentrate on the passing episode as if it were the last work, as if the curtain dropped on Him with disaster and defeat? That dreadful scene lasted a few hours. But to the unending eternity, Christ is alive; the stone has been rolled away, and He rules and reigns and triumphs![3]

The empty tomb determines what Easter is. Here is what we must remember and defend: heaven celebrates the resurrection. Hell fears the resurrection, and the rest of us just look for our car keys wanting to be first out of the parking lot out of a crowded church.

Mary just finishes speaking to the resurrected Jesus, and she is now telling the disciples about her experience at the tomb. She saw a stone door couldn't stop Him, and now they learn neither can their locked doors.

The closed-door conversation is recorded in John 20:18–20 (NASB):

> **18** Mary Magdalene *came, announcing to the
> disciples, "I have seen the Lord," and that He had
> said these things to her. **19** So when it was evening
> on that day, the first day of the week, and when the
> doors were shut where the disciples were, for fear of
> the Jews, Jesus came and stood in their midst and
> *said to them, "Peace be with you." **20** And when
> He had said this, He showed them both His hands
> and His side. The disciples then rejoiced when they
> saw the Lord.

What does the resurrection mean?

It means no door can keep Jesus out. Those doors can be big, locked, and guarded. It doesn't matter. Jesus goes where He wants to.

Just try telling Jesus He can't come into your world.

He will go into any campus frat house, locker rooms, city pubs and clubs, bars, office buildings, and private universities. He will enter into penthouses and crack houses and even the White House. The Risen Christ does not know the barricades of locked doors or locked hearts. The Risen Christ is not limited by our closed windows or closed minds. No atheist is safe. No skeptic is hidden, and no person is off limits. He doesn't just wait for you to come to church. He can show up anywhere.

He has proven that from day one of His resurrection.

Writer Peter Larsen said, "Despite our efforts to keep him out, God intrudes. The life of Jesus is bracketed by two impossibilities: 'a virgin's womb and an empty tomb.' Jesus entered our world through a door marked, 'No Entrance' and left through a door marked 'No Exit.'"[4]

If He can rise from the dead, I think He can break through any worldview, any mindset, or any family curse or prejudice you may have set up. Set up a barrier and He will walk through it. Jesus stands among the disciples, and the words before that say, "The doors were shut."

A man and his five-year-old son were driving past a cemetery and noticed a large pile of dirt next to a freshly dug grave when the little boy said, "Look, Dad, one got out!"

Next time you drive past a cemetery, think of the One whom the grave could not hold. An empty grave on that Easter morning tells us about our graves.

Jesus said in John 14:19 (NIV), "Because I live, you also will live."

That grave did not hold Him, and it will not hold us.

Hallelujah!

MY PRAYER FOR TODAY:

Father, I know so many people who have locked You out. Now, I know that is no threat to You. You have shown us, over and over again, that You can show up in places that have locked You out. Now, I realize there is no such thing as a closed country to the gospel message. I wish those nations knew about gravestones and locked doors.

1. Jon Stewart, *The Daily Show*, "Tweets from Tahrir: Egypt's Revolution as it Unfolded, in the Words of the People who Made It," season 16, episode 11, Comedy Central, April 25, 2011.

2. Arnold Toynbee, Man's Concern with Death (1969), as quoted in Charles Swindoll, *The Tale of the Tardy Oxcart* (Nashville: W Publishing Group, 1998), 318.

3. Note that Michelangelo is believed to have said this quote during the High Renaissance period, likely sometime in the early sixteenth century, although the exact date is not definitively recorded; it is often attributed to a conversation he had with fellow artists regarding the prevalent theme of Christ on the Cross in art at the time.

4. According to a piece in *The Sudbury Star*, Peter Larson said, "Despite our efforts to keep him out, God intrudes. The life of Jesus is bracketed by two impossibilities: a virgin's womb and an empty tomb. Jesus entered our world through a door marked, 'No Entrance' and left through a door marked 'No Exit.'" However, the exact date of when he said this is not provided in the search results.

It's important to note that this quote is often attributed to Mark Cahill as well, suggesting that both individuals may have expressed this or a similar sentiment. Further research might be needed to determine the precise date and authorship.

DAY 27

Check the Rock

Some years ago, a letter appeared in the national news that was sent to a deceased person by the Indiana Department of Social Services. As the story goes, it read as follows: "Dear Madam, Your food stamps will be stopped effective March 1st because we received notice that you passed away. Our deepest sympathies for your family. You may reapply if there is a change in your circumstances."

There haven't been too many who have seen a change in those kind of circumstances. Well, there was one person: Jesus!

What is Easter? The simplest meaning of Easter is that we are living in a world in which God has the last word. John Stott said it like this, "We live and die; Christ died and lives."[1]

There is something exciting when you speak about the resurrected Jesus to others. When you speak about Jesus and about all the other religious leaders, they part ways when you use verbs after their names. To all the other religious leaders of the past, you have to add "ed" to all their verbs. You say Mohammed lived and Joseph Smith walked. It's all in the past tense!

Jesus is in a class all by Himself. Because of the resurrection, Jesus' verbs end in "s." A present-tense verb ends in "s," which means the action is happening right now! We can say Jesus speaks, Jesus walks, Jesus heals, Jesus delivers, and Jesus saves. I'll take the one with the "s" on the end of His verbs over all the other religions.

It was missionary David Seamands who tells us of a Muslim who became a Christian in China, and he tells this story:

> Some of his friends asked him, "Why have you become a Christian?" He answered, "Well, it's like this. Suppose you were going down the road and suddenly the road forked in two directions, and you didn't know which way to go, and there at the fork in the road were two men, one dead and one alive,— which one would you ask which way should I go? Ask the guy who is alive."[2]

That means you choose the guy whose verbs end in "s."

The resurrected Jesus changes everything! All you have to do today is look in the right direction. To have people without resurrection life trying to solve life's problems is futile.

Three women were discussing a problem with the answer in front of them. Three women who were so set on their assignment, they almost missed the miracle! They came to the tomb and never thought they would leave with a resurrected Christ.

Mark 16:1–4 (NASB) says,

> **1** When the Sabbath was over, Mary Magdalene, and Mary the mother of James, and Salome, bought spices, so that they might come and anoint Him.
> **2** Very early in the morning, on the first day of the week, they came to the tomb when the sun had

risen. 3 They were saying to one another, "Who will
roll away the stone for us from the entrance of the
tomb?" 4 Looking up, they saw that the stone had
been rolled away.

Those three women asked the question, "Who will roll away the stone for us?" but they never looked up and realized it was already done for them. They were asking a question that God had already answered for them! They never looked up and realized it was already done for them. They were asking a question that God had already answered

What was their assignment and task? They were coming to make a dead man smell better. They were fooling around with spices and smelly stuff for a corpse.

It was Easter Day of 1960, and William Sangster, one of Britian's leading preachers, lay dying in his home in London. He was in his last stages of a paralyzing disease of MS. He could not speak a word nor walk a step.

His sole means of communication with his loved ones was pencil and pad. On that day, he slowly picked them up and painfully penned these wonderful words: "Easter Day! What a pity not to be able to shout on Easter Day."

Then, for a little while, he paused. He later added, "But what a tragedy if you have nothing to shout about on Easter."[3]

These three women almost missed a shouting moment. When you don't see what God has done, you end up living a life of managing tragedy and hardship instead of victory. You do your best to make dead things smell good.

The three of them were not meant to anoint His dead body. They were meant to tell others that He's alive! That was their real assignment.

The angel said to them in Mark 16:6–7 (NASB), "He has risen; He is not here; behold, here is the place where they laid Him. But go, tell His disciples."

An empty tomb changes our lives and our purpose! Instead of sprinkling scented spices on dead things, you realize there is more to life. They almost missed it because they didn't check the rock.

In a state park in California there is a rock hanging on a rope with a large sign next to it. The sign says "Weather Report: Check the Rock," and at first glance, it seems infantile but, in actuality, it is genius. The weather report rock sign goes on to say, "If it's wet, then it's raining. If the rock is swinging, then it's windy. If the rock is white, it's snowing; if the rock is dry, then it's not raining. If you cannot see the rock, it's foggy; if the rock is missing and has been blown away, it's a tornado."[4]

This is incredible. This is Easter!

The issue with these three women is that they didn't check the rock!

On that cross, Jesus didn't say, "I am finished." He said, "It is finished," because He was just getting started!

MY PRAYER FOR TODAY

Father, don't let me miss the obvious miracles in front of me every day. Those women almost missed the empty tomb because they were looking down instead of up. Today, I start with my head up, seeing that every day, there are miracles all around me. There are heavy stones You are moving for me each day.

1. See Quote Fancy, in "John R. W. Stott Quotes," accessed February 23, 2025, https://quotefancy.com/quote/1432386/John-R-W-Stott-We-live-and-die-Christ-died-and-lived.

2. David A. Seamands, *Healing for Damaged Emotions* (Colorado Springs: David C. Cook, 2015), Kindle.

3. Roy B. Zuck, *The Speaker's Quote Book: Over 5,000 Illustrations and Quotations for All Occasions* (Grand Rapids, MI: Kregel Publications), 63.

4. See "Weather rock," *Wikipedia*, last modified February 16, 2025, https://en.wikipedia.org/wiki/Weather_rock#References.

DAY 28

Smoke Damage

The five senses (touch, smell, sight, hearing, and taste) not only assess the present, but they also have a connection to the past. They say that the sense of smell provides the most vivid recollection of the past of all the five senses.[1]

I remember my friend Richard and I went one day as teenagers to pick up his parents from the airport. I will never forget coming home in the car with Richard and his parents and seeing his house completely on fire. It was devastating.

When the fire was finally put out, I remember walking through the house with him, seeing what survived. Though the house did not burn to the ground, there were some things that, though they survived the flames, didn't survive the excessive smoke and were smoke damaged. The smoke damage was extensive.

I remember all his clothes and guitars smelled like a house fire for a long time. Every time he came to church, the smell reminded me of that night. Honestly, every time I have been in the vicinity of a house fire, the odor simulates my memory and takes me back decades.

There was another fire after the resurrection that brought back a tragic memory. Before the crucifixion, Peter made this huge promise to Jesus and said, "Though all deny You, Jesus, I will never deny You."

Many know what happened after the promise but have missed the fire.

The Gospel of John tells us in John 18:15–18 (NASB):

> **15** Simon Peter was following Jesus, and so was
> another disciple. Now that disciple was known to the
> high priest, and entered with Jesus into the court of
> the high priest, **16** but Peter was standing at the door
> outside. So the other disciple, who was known to the
> high priest, went out and spoke to the doorkeeper,
> and brought Peter in. **17** Then the slave-girl who
> kept the door said to Peter, "You are not also one of
> this man's disciples, are you?" He said, "I am not."
> **18** Now the slaves and the officers were standing
> there, having made a charcoal fire, for it was cold
> and they were warming themselves; and Peter was
> also with them, standing and warming himself.

Charcoal makes me think of holiday weekend barbecues, but for Peter, it makes him think the worst day of his life. Why? It reminded him of one thing . . . his betrayal.

Peter was dealing with smoke damage. I have to believe that Peter's sense of smell did to him what a house fire did to me. I bet charcoal was a trigger switch that brought him back to that fateful night of failure. How could this be fixed? It will be fixed by the resurrected Jesus.

Jesus is alive, and Peter was freshly off his denial tour. The two are going to meet again on the beach at the Sea of Galilee.

Peter is fishing (because he thinks it's all over), and Jesus is standing on the beach. Then, something happens: John and Peter recognize Jesus from their fishing boat.

John 21:7–8 says,

> **7** Therefore that disciple whom Jesus loved said to Peter, "It is the Lord." So when Simon Peter heard that it was the Lord, he put his outer garment on (for he was stripped for work), and threw himself into the sea. **8** But the other disciples came in the little boat, for they were not far from the land, but about one hundred yards away, dragging the net full of fish.

Instead of Peter hiding like Adam, Peter jumps in the water and swims one hundred yards to his healing. Peter is swimming and is excited Jesus is alive and on the beach cooking breakfast.

After he swims four Olympic-size pool laps, he dries off on the sand, and is hit in the face with an odor that takes him to a dark place.

What is that smell? Peter thought.

John 21:9 tells us, "So when they got out on the land, they saw a charcoal fire already laid and fish placed on it, and bread."

Charcoal? No! Jesus couldn't have used propane? The last thing Peter ever wanted to smell again was charcoal.

It was over a charcoal fire that three denials took place when Peter said, "I never knew Him."

Charcoal memories are failures to the fisherman. He is meeting Jesus for the first time after the resurrection . . . with charcoal in the air! His ears hear Jesus talking. His eyes see the resurrected Jesus. But his nose smells charcoal: the equivalent of failure, fear, rejection, and denial.

Why the charcoal fire, Jesus? You knew what happened? Was Jesus rubbing it in?

I don't think so. We don't understand breakfast in the Middle East in the first century.

John tells us what comes next in John 21:10–12:

> **10** Jesus said to them, "Bring some of the fish which you have now caught." **11** Simon Peter went up and drew the net to land, full of large fish, a hundred and fifty-three; and although there were so many, the net was not torn. **12** Jesus said to them, "Come and have breakfast."

"Come and have breakfast" were second-chance words. A meal in the Middle East was incredibly significant because you never ate with your enemy, you only ate with your friends. You only ate with those whom you were in close relationship to.

When Jesus said, "Come and have breakfast," I believe those were the first words of the resurrected Jesus to Peter personally. He heard other things Jesus said, but those were His words. Come have breakfast meant "You are my friends. All other religions are you wanting God, but Christianity is God wanting you!" And Jesus wanted Peter back.

We are told in the book of Revelation that when anyone wants to have a relationship with God, that person is invited to a spiritual meal.

John, who was the other fisherman, wrote these words in Revelation 3:20 (NLT): "I stand at the door and knock. If you hear my voice and open the door, I will come in, and we will share a meal together as friends."

That meal was saying, "Peter, we are friends! We are going to fix the past and change your future."

MY PRAYER FOR TODAY

Father, there are a lot of things that remind me of my failures. There are a lot of charcoal fires burning every day to tell me that my past is unforgivable, making me unusable. I thank You that You fight fire with fire. You cooked breakfast on charcoal to give a new memory to Peter. You were reminding him and me: You call us to a table of friendship to heal the past so that we both can change the future.

1. "Psychology and Smell," accessed February 10, 2025, Fifth Sense, https://www.fifthsense.org.uk/psychology-and-smell/#:~:text=The%20sense%20of%20smell%20is,any%20of%20our%20other%20senses.

DAY 29

Just When You Want to Give Up, There's a Day Eight

There is a cartoon I saw some time ago. I believe it was from *The Animated Bible Series*, but I'm not positive. The gist of it is below:

A few of the disciples were standing around the tomb where Jesus was buried. They looked surprised at the stone that was moved. And then one of them pulls out a scroll and says, "Oh wait, He changed His status. He's risen. That's why He's not here."

It's totally true with just some updated language. Jesus' status changed three days after being buried in a tomb. Someone who did not get the memo of this status change was Thomas. Thomas missed the resurrected Jesus when He showed up at the disciples' closed-door meeting.

John tells us that on resurrection evening, Jesus showed up. He says in John 20:19–20 (NRSV),

> **19** When therefore it was evening, on that day, the first day of the week, and when the doors were shut where the disciples were, for fear of the Jews, Jesus came and stood in their midst, and said to them,

> "Peace be with you." **20** And when He had said this,
> He showed them both His hands and His side. The
> disciples therefore rejoiced when they saw the Lord.

Jesus showed up and showed ten of them His wounded hands and side, and then they rejoiced with Him.

John continues on to tell us about the encounter and gives us this attendance record in verse 24 (KJB): "But Thomas, one of the twelve, called Didymus, was not with them when Jesus came."

There were only ten disciples at that encounter. The betrayer has died, and the doubter has gone MIA. Talk about missing it. Thomas missed it big time.

There is good news for Thomas, however. Jesus never gives up on us. That good news is recorded in John 20:26–28 (NASB) just a little further in the story. It's a reminder to all of us that just when we want to give up on someone, God always has a day eight:

> **26** After eight days His disciples were again inside,
> and Thomas with them. Jesus *came, the doors
> having been shut, and stood in their midst and said,
> "Peace be with you." **27** Then He *said to Thomas,
> "Reach here with your finger, and see My hands; and
> reach here your hand and put it into My side; and
> do not be unbelieving, but believing." **28** Thomas
> answered and said to Him, "My Lord and my God!"

Thomas got to rejoice. Thomas got to dissolve his doubts. Thomas met Jesus because Thomas got a day eight. Day eight means don't give hope; God is not done.

Some people need to only hear a word, and some people need more time. Thomas needed both. He needed a word from Jesus and eight more days. And God gave it to him.

It took more power from God to save the world than to create the world. The Bible calls creation in Psalm 8:3 (TLB) "the work of His fingers." But Isaiah in 59:16 (NASB) says, "His own arm brought salvation. . . ."

Think about it: it takes more work to redeem man then it does to create the heavens and the earth. Creation just needed His fingers, but salvation needed His arm. It may have taken the arms of God to help Thomas, but praise God that He is willing to extend His arms to us.

Thank You, God, for going the distance for us, even when we are more work for Him than creating a universe! God puts in the work to get you to salvation.

Don't be disheartened, the resurrected Jesus is also the patient Jesus. This missed encounter has a message for us. It's a message of hope. You missed the event of human history and now what, Thomas?

We don't know why Thomas wasn't there, but we can guess. We can surmise based on his nickname, "doubting Thomas." I don't think we are off base to conclude that Thomas is not at the resurrection evening service because he just doubts that a resurrection even happened. His doubting prevented him from rejoicing.

But Thank God for His patience. He is patient with doubters and the dense. He is patient with those who miss it and even those who reject His resurrection. He will come at the right time because He loves you.

You may be a Christian, and you may have family members who are not, and their lack of belief and doubts may vex you. You want them so badly to meet the resurrected Jesus.

Thomas the doubter turning into Thomas the believer gives us hope. Your skeptical family members may be eight-days-later believers as well. For them, it may take another encounter and a different encounter than you have experienced. Personally, I am so thankful for Thomas' conversion story because it calms my heart for those I love that don't know Jesus yet.

Maybe you are reading this now and you have not experienced the resurrected Jesus. These simple words may be day eight for you. This may be the moment you say with Thomas, "My Lord and my God."

MY PRAYER FOR TODAY

Father, thank You for eight days later. Thank You for Your patience with people who have missed You. I must remember that my loved ones may not be in church and that they may be missing God showing up, but it's not over. You are the God of day eight. Thank You that while, at times, I have given up on them, You have not.

DAY 30

Now Comes the Good Part

Some years ago, I read a story about a particular family who was watching the Easter story on television. Although the entire family had seen the movie before, one little girl was particularly moved by the movie. As Jesus was tortured and crucified, tears came streaming down her cheek. She remained completely silent, with the exception of a few sobs, until they put Jesus' body into the tomb. At that point, she suddenly smiled and then shouted, "Now comes the good part!"

Theologian Gerald O'Collins puts it this way: "Christianity without the resurrection is not simply Christianity without its final chapter. It is not Christianity at all."[1]

The resurrection is the good part, the best part, the main part. What has captivated me is what Jesus would say after He defeated death. There are many sermons and books on the seven words of Jesus from the cross. These words explain the purpose of the cross and the character of Christ. But what is ignored is the first seven words of the Risen Savior after the resurrection. The seven words of the cross give a message from God to all the world. But the first seven words of the Risen Christ give a message from God to the Church and to his people.

Be encouraged as you hear some of the words of the resurrected Jesus.

Jesus speaks to tears and to a woman first. His first words are in John 20:15 (NASB): "Jesus said to her, 'Woman, why are you weeping?'"

Jesus is telling Mary, you shouldn't be crying, you should be shouting. The answer to your tears is a resurrected Jesus. Don't let tears replace the shout. Jesus conquered death.

Then Jesus speaks her name, "Mary," in John 20:15–16:

> **15** Supposing Him to be the gardener, she *said to Him, "Sir, if you have carried Him away, tell me where you have laid Him, and I will take Him away."
> **16** Jesus *said to her, "Mary!"

He knows your name. Mary thought Jesus was the gardener. She did not realize she was speaking to the Creator of the garden. And the Creator would say her name.

Remember, you are not a number, and you are not defined by your failures. Jesus tells us from the moment He resurrects that He knows Mary and He knows you. Just when you feel like God doesn't care, listen for the whisper, and you will hear Him say your name.

Jesus would not allow this to be an event only, this was the message. He tells Mary in John 20:17: "go to My brethren and say to them, 'I ascend to My Father and your Father, and My God and your God.'"

He tells her, we have a story to tell: If you cling to Me, then others can't hear it. Let go and start shouting it from the housetops. Jesus is alive!

In a world of chaos, Jesus comes and speaks to His disciples for the first time and says in John 20:19: "Peace be with you."

His first words to His disciples is peace. What a word! You have failed in your promises. You have slept when you should have been praying. You fled when you should have stayed. You got scared when you should have trusted. And to all of this, Jesus said peace. To anyone (and everyone) who feels they let God down, He speaks peace right out of the gate.

Jesus then equips them to tell this message. He says in John 20:21–22:

> **21** "as the Father has sent Me, I also send you."
> **22** And when He had said this, He breathed on them and said to them, "Receive the Holy Spirit. You are not alone. As I was sent with the Holy Spirit, you too will be sent the same way."

Jesus will speak to the unbelieving. While men rejoiced over this day, one man was still processing and doubting. His name was Thomas. Jesus found him as recorded in John 20:27: "Then He *said to Thomas, 'Reach here with your finger, and see My hands; and reach here your hand and put it into My side; and do not be unbelieving, but believing.'"

The unbelieving is part of His mission. Jesus wants unbelievers to be believers. These are words of hope.

Jesus speaks to those in the future and says in John 20:29: "Blessed are they who did not see, and yet believed."

That's us. We are faith people, and we are blessed people. God pronounces blessing on those who will walk with the resurrected Jesus by faith.

Think of the words of the resurrected Jesus and receive them as a comfort, a challenge, and a commission. Jesus wipes our tears away. Jesus calls our name. Jesus commissions us to tell the good news. He gives peace to those who feel they have failed God. He equips them with the Holy Spirit and power. He will replace unbelief with belief. And He will bless the person of faith.

Think of the content: tears, a name, go tell, peace, Holy Spirit, believe, and blessing. These are the words of the resurrected Christ for us in the Gospel of John, but they are much more than words.

The Resurrection of Christ was the miracle of miracles. Without it, He is not a Savior. Without the resurrection, there is no salvation. Without the resurrection, there is no hope beyond the grave. And without the resurrection, He is a liar.

Hallelujah, Jesus is alive. We have all that He is promised and everything He said is true. Every word that was said can be taken to the bank.

MY PRAYER FOR TODAY

Father, I rejoice that You are alive. And I rejoice that You have something to tell Your church. You did not leave us without a word, but You have given us everything we need to change the world.

1. Gerald O'Collins, *The Easter Jesus* (London: Darton, Longman & Todd, 1973), 134.

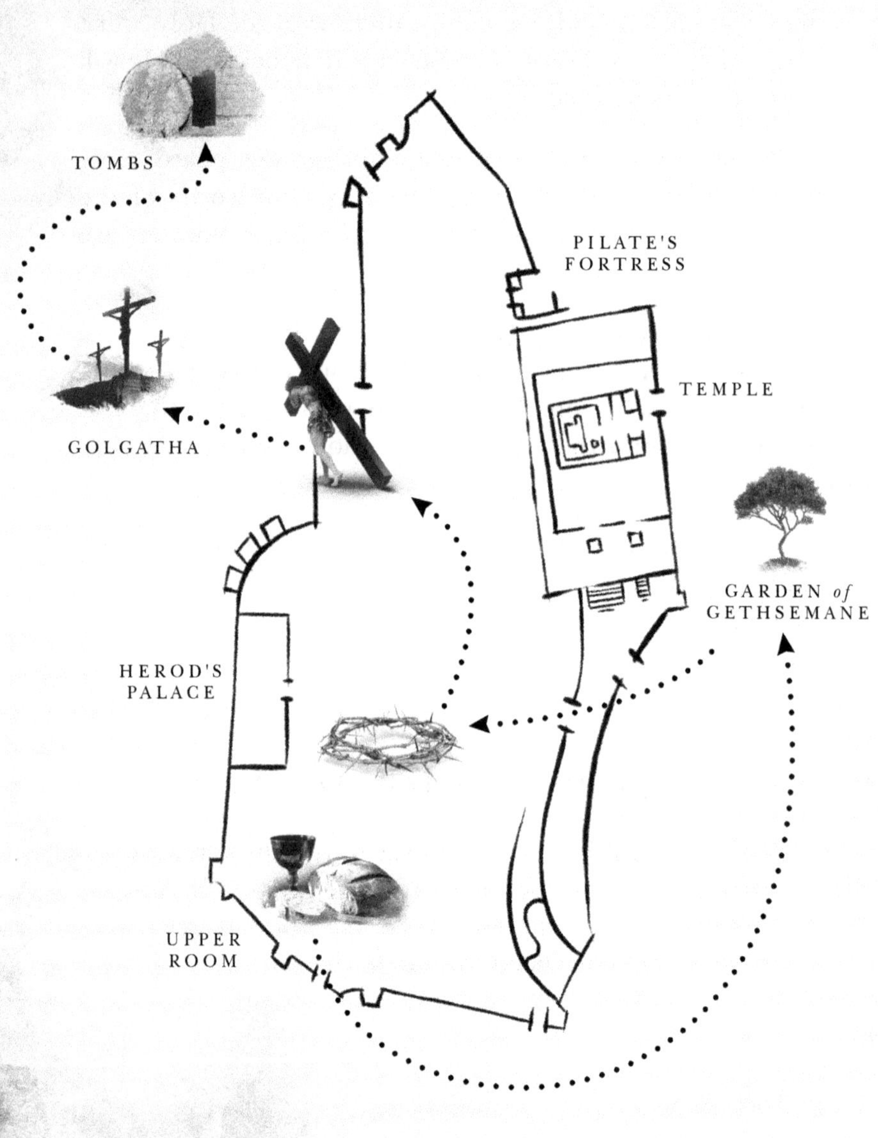
TOMBS
PILATE'S
FORTRESS
TEMPLE
GOLGATHA
GARDEN of
GETHSEMANE
HEROD'S
PALACE
UPPER
ROOM

EPILOGUE

FINAL WORDS

FINAL WORDS

What Does This All Mean?

When God raised Jesus from the dead, why didn't God fix His body?

Why did God the Father leave the scars on God the Son? Why would the print of nails still be there so Thomas could feel them with his fingers? Can it be that the resurrection is saying to all of us: "You can live life with your greatest wounds and you can go forward though you have scars?" Does it remind us that the resurrection of Jesus means that the worst thing is never the last thing?

Somehow, we must understand that the resurrected Christ is forever the wounded Christ. He is living but yet marked with human evil. He will reign as King forever yet scarred for eternity.

Every Sunday at our church, I love looking to my right from the stage. There before me is our Times Square Church Deaf Ministry.

The deaf have a sign for the name of Jesus. The middle finger of each hand is placed into the palm of the other hand. When they do this action, they are saying Jesus by describing Him as the One with wounded hands. When they touch that palm, they remember. They hear the name in their own flesh. Those nail scars remind them—and us—the reason why He came.

All that the Son of God did was for you. His walk to the cross and His scars from the cross were done for you. The pain He felt was so you could experience forgiveness and heaven.

When I hear people tell me that they can get to heaven by being a good person, I am shocked. If that was the case, then all that Jesus was sent to experience was the worst case of child abuse in human history. So God the Father sent His Son to be mocked, beaten, scourged, scarred, tortured, and killed and then tell humanity "you must live a good life to get to heaven"? That doesn't even make sense. His death meant something. His suffering meant something. His resurrection still means something. It means we can't get to heaven without God's help. He sent Jesus to help us get home, our eternal home.

Today, would you accept the fact that all that was described in this book was done for you to get you to heaven? If you would believe that, then today can change the rest of your life . . . and the rest of your forever.

Today, you can start a journey with God. You may protest, "Wait, I have to fix some things in my life so God would like me better!" But here is the good news and the real news: God doesn't like you. God loves you. And the cross is the proof of that.

Today, accept that His death was for your sins. Accept that He rose from the dead so that you might live forever. Accept that God's Son was on that cross bearing your sins. Receive His forgiveness and begin a brand-new life.

PRAY THIS PRAYER WITH ME

Thank You, Jesus, for coming to earth for me.
Thank You, Jesus, for going to the cross for me.
Thank You, Jesus, for suffering in my place.
Thank You, Jesus, for rising from the dead and defeating death for me.
Today, come and change me from the inside out.
I accept the fact that I can't get myself to heaven, and I need You in my life.
You are God. You are Lord. You are alive.
I receive You into my life.

Amen

STRENGTHEN PEOPLE'S FAITH

Help others find this book.

1

Post a picture on your social media and share why you found it meaningful.

2

Gift it to someone who might benefit from it.

3

Go through it with a friend, or start a Bible study group.

Thank you for helping people rediscover the awe of Jesus' death and resurrection!

ALSO AVAILABLE

FROM TIM DILENA

GET INSIGHT

Discover life-changing lessons from each New Testament chapter, one day at a time.

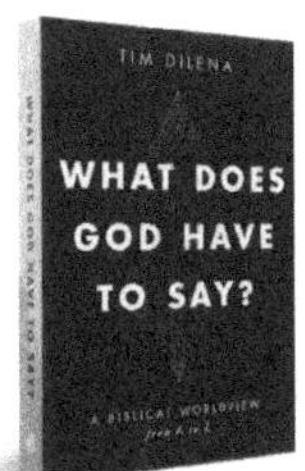

STAND FIRM

Learn God's principles to hold steady in an unstable world.

TRUST GOD

See how God led others through life's ups and downs.

LEARN TO PRAY

Discover 101 ways to talk to God about your struggles, like fear, forgiveness, anxiety and more.

DON'T GIVE UP

Nurture a daily mindset to keep you moving forward in life and in faith.

BREAK THROUGH

Experience how the power of prayer can change everything.

For more spiritual insight to help you thrive in everyday life:

Explore
messages and books at
tsc.nyc

Follow us

@TimesSquareChurch

@PastorTimDilena

www.ingramcontent.com/pod-product-compliance
Lightning Source LLC
Jackson TN
JSHW080053120126
96429JS00001B/1
* 9 7 8 1 9 5 6 3 7 0 8 8 1 *